Social Work and the Law in Scotland

Social Work and the Law in Scotland

Janet Fabb BA, DIPSW, CQSW
Lecturer in Social Work at the University of Paisley

Thomas G Guthrie LLB (HONS)
Lecturer in Law at the University of Glasgow

Edinburgh
Butterworths
1992

United Kingdom	Butterworth & Co (Publishers) Ltd, 4 Hill Street, EDINBURGH EH2 3JZ, 88 Kingsway, LONDON WC2B 6AB
Australia	Butterworths Pty Ltd, SYDNEY, MELBOURNE, BRISBANE, ADELAIDE, PERTH, CANBERRA and HOBART
Belgium	Butterworth & Co (Publishers) Ltd, BRUSSELS
Canada	Butterworths Canada Ltd, TORONTO and VANCOUVER
Ireland	Butterworth (Ireland) Ltd, DUBLIN
Malaysia	Malayan Law Journal Sdn Bhd, KUALA LUMPUR
New Zealand	Butterworths of New Zealand Ltd, WELLINGTON and AUCKLAND
Puerto Rico	Equity de Puerto Rico, Inc, HATO REY
Singapore	Butterworth & Co (Asia) Pte Ltd, SINGAPORE
USA	Butterworth Legal Publishers, ST PAUL, Minnesota; SEATTLE, Washington; BOSTON, Massachusetts; AUSTIN, Texas and D & S Publishers, CLEARWATER, Florida

Reprinted 1993

A CIP Catalogue record for this book is available from the British Library.

ISBN 0 406 12123 0

Typeset by Phoenix Photosetting, Chatham, Kent
Printed in Great Britain by Latimer Trend & Company Ltd, Plymouth, Devon

Preface

This book is intended to serve as a good place to start learning or reviewing social work and the law in Scotland. It is not meant as a good place to end the process. We have chosen to include a broad selection of topics which comprise the core of the subject and to offer direction to pursue topics in depth elsewhere. Our primary aim is to enable the reader to gain an understanding of the legal framework within which social work is practised in Scotland, and to facilitate the acquisition or review of specific legal knowledge necessary to make sense of most day-to-day social work practice.

A secondary aim is to provide one basic text which covers the most commonly encountered areas of law for social workers in Scotland in a way which will serve as a ready reference. Often there is a confusion about what is law, what is policy, what are procedures, and what is the status of each and so another aim is to clarify the law and its status and thus distinguish the law from policy and procedures.

Social work students and social workers need to know the law as it relates to their practice, but increasingly there are others who have an interest in this selection of topics; solicitors, sheriffs, children's panel members, safeguarders, curators, guardians, reporters, doctors, health visitors, community psychiatric nurses, occupational therapists, teachers, parents, young adults, children and others. Social work is touching more lives and an informed contact is always preferable. We have attempted to avoid being prescriptive since this seems to us to invite reductionist thinking, could well be wrong, and does little to value the experience of the reader. Sometimes, however, the material is best served by some limited prescription and we hope it will be accepted in the spirit in which it is written. We have sought to offer suggestions which highlight the unique and specific opportunities, constraints, and responsibilities for social workers in this context rather than an exhaustive programme for all social work involvement.

This book is based very closely on a course for qualifying social workers which has evolved over the past seven years at Paisley College (now the University of Paisley). We were the staff primarily responsible for the curriculum development and the teaching of this course. One of us brings a social work background and one a legal background to the work and in some sense the text exhibits graphically the tensions experienced between these two professions.

Our thanks are due to the current social work practitioners who participated in the teaching of the course and directed us to what was relevant from the point of view of practice and to our social work students and graduates who have given invaluable feedback in the development of the material. Particular thanks are due to our colleagues for making some space and time for us and especially to Harry Brooks, Iain Ferguson and Alison Robertson for their comments and contributions. The responsibility for any errors and infelicities in expression remains, of course, ours.

Finally, and most importantly, thanks are due to our respective families for their support and understanding.

We have attempted to state the law and practice issues as at 31 July 1992 though we have anticipated changes in the level of fines which take effect from 1 October 1992. No attempt has been made to anticipate the proposals of the expected White Paper on child care law, which could result in substantial changes to the law at some uncertain time in the future.

Where we refer to particular sections of Acts of Parliament we have referred only to the section of the original or principal Act. Readers should be aware that in many cases the provisions of the original Act will have been subsequently amended; for the sake of simplicity we have not referred to the amending legislation. One example of this process is, of course, the Social Work (Scotland) Act 1968 which has been amended by (amongst others) the Children Act 1975 and the Health and Social Services Act 1983.

Janet Fabb
Tom Guthrie

Glasgow

Contents

Table of statutes

Table of cases

Further reading

CHAPTER 1

E A Marshall & R Gray	*The Social Work (Scotland) Act 1968* (2nd edn, 1984, Greens)

CHAPTER 2

CPAG	*National Welfare Benefits Handbook* (published annually)
CPAG	*Rights Guide to Non-means Tested Benefits* (published annually)
G Fimister	*Welfare Rights Work in Social Services* (1986, Macmillan/ CPAG)
A McAllister	*Scottish Law of Leases* (Chs 13, 14) (1989, Butterworths)
I Macdonald & N Blake	*Immigration Law and Practice* (3rd edn, 1991, Butterworths)
D Pannick	*Sex Discrimination Law* (1985, Oxford Clarendon)
P Pearce et al	*Personal Data Protection in Health and Social Services* (1988)
Scottish Consumer Council	*The Law of the School* (1987, HMSO)
Scottish Homeless Group	*Homelessness – Your Rights* (4th edn, 1991)

Scottish Office Environment Department — *Homelessness – Part II of the Housing (Scotland) Act 1987: Code of Guidance – Scotland* (1991)

G & J Stewart — *Boundary Changes – Social Work and Social Security* (1986, CPAG/BASW)

P Watchman & P Robson — *Homelessness and the Law in Britain* (2nd edn, 1989, Planning Exchange)

CHAPTER 3

A Mitchell — *Children in the Middle* (1985, Tavistock)

L Parkinson — *Conciliation in Separation & Divorce* (1986)

J M Thomson — *Family Law in Scotland* (2nd edn, 1991, Butterworths)

J S Wallerstein & J B Kelly — *Surviving the Break-up* (1980, Grant McIntyre)

CHAPTER 4

R M Adler — *Taking Juvenile Justice Seriously* (1985, Scottish Academic Press)

S Asquith — *Children and Justice* (1983, Edinburgh University Press)

B Kahan — *Child Care Research Policy and Practice* (1989, Hodder & Stoughton/OUP)

B Kearney — *Children's Hearings and the Sheriff Court* (1987, Butterworths)

A Maluccio et al — *Permanency Planning for Children* (1986, Tavistock)

F M Martin & K Murray — *The Scottish Juvenile Justice System* (1982, Scottish Academic Press)

G Moore — *A Guide to the Children's Hearings* (1989, Greens)

Scottish Child and Family Alliance — *In The Child's Best Interests* (1991, HMSO)

Scottish Office — *Review of Child Care Law in Scotland* (1990, HMSO)

J Thoburn — *Child Placement: Principles and Practice* (1988, Wildwood House)

CHAPTER 5

D Anderson — *Social Work and Mental Handicap* (1982, Macmillan)

J Blackie et al — *Mental Health: A Guide to the Law in Scotland* (1990, Butterworths/Scottish Legal Education Trust)

R Griffith — *Community Care – an Agenda for Action* (1988, HMSO)

M Marshall — *Social Work with Old People* (2nd edn, 1990, Macmillan)

M Oliver — *The Politics of Disablement* (1991, Macmillan)

M Oliver — *Social Work with Disabled People* (1983)

Scottish Action on Dementia — *Dementia: Money and Legal Matters* (1991)

Scottish Home and Health Dept — *Code of Practice: Mental Health (Scotland) Act 1984* (1990)

A Ward — *Scots Law and the Mentally Handicapped* (1984, Scottish Society for the Mentally Handicapped)

A Ward — *The Power to Act* (1990, Scottish Society for the Mentally Handicapped)

CHAPTER 6

J Blackie et al	*Mental Health: A Guide to the Law in Scotland* (1990, Butterworths/Scottish Legal Education Trust) (Ch 5)
H Blagg & D Smith	*Crime, Penal Policy and Social Work* (1989, Longman)
P Carlen & A Worrall	*Gender, Crime and Justice* (1987, Open University Press)
A Coyle	*Inside. Rethinking Scotland's Prisons* (1991, Scottish Child)
R E & R Dobash & S Gutteridge	*The Imprisonment of Women* (1986, Basil Blackwell)
C Fishwick	*Court Work* (2nd edn, 1989, PEPAR)
T May	*Probation: Politics, Policy and Practice* (1990, Open University Press)
G Moore & C Wood	*Social Work and Criminal Law in Scotland* (1981) and Update (1987, Aberdeen University Press)
C G B Nicholson	*The Law and Practice of Sentencing in Scotland* (1981) and Supplement (1985, Greens)
J Pitts	*Working with Young Offenders* (1990, Macmillan)
P Raynor	*Social Work, Justice and Control* (1985, Basil Blackwell)
Scottish Office	*National Objectives and Standards for Social Work Services in the Criminal Justice System* (1991)
A L Stewart	*The Scottish Criminal Courts in Action* (1990, Butterworths)
H Walker & B Beaumont (eds)	*Working with Offenders* (1985, Basil Blackwell)

List of abbreviations

CASE REPORTS

All ER	All England Law Reports
GWD	Greens Weekly Digest
SCLR	Scottish Civil Law Reports
SLT	Scots Law Times Reports
SLT (Sh Ct)	Scots Law Times Sheriff Court Reports

STATUTES

The 1968 Act	The Social Work (Scotland) Act 1968
The 1984 Act	The Mental Health (Scotland) Act 1984

OTHER

BASW	British Association of Social Workers
CCETSW	Central Council for the Education and Training in Social Work
HC	House of Commons Papers
SCOLAG	Scottish Legal Action Group

1. The Scottish legal context of social work

1. INTRODUCTION

EXAMPLE

Martin, aged 15, is a young man who has been referred to a children's hearing on the grounds of having committed an offence – theft from a shop in the town centre. His mother, Linda, is a lone parent who is financially dependent upon state benefit and has a very unreliable social support network. A social worker arranges to visit with each of them in order to prepare a social background report for the reporter and, if the family are agreeable, to assess fully their needs and level of social functioning with a view to future work together.

Most social work in Scotland is practised within the context of local authority social work departments. This text will concentrate on this framework except where special reference is made to the voluntary or private sector. There is a legal dimension to all of the work undertaken by such social workers.

Social workers are **obliged** to perform some functions and **permitted** to perform others by the laws passed by parliament and arising out of court cases. They also have specified **powers** and **duties** which are defined by the law and derive much of their authority from the law. Martin, Linda and other people in contact with social workers employed by the local authority have specified **rights** and **responsibilities** which are based in law. The contact between Martin and Linda and the social worker is therefore driven by the law and without a basic knowledge of that law the social worker cannot function competently and the client may also forfeit various legal entitlements.

Social workers need to be able to recognise and make use of this legal dimension in social work practice. For example, the social worker must understand that he/she has a duty to supply the reporter with relevant information about Martin, Linda, and their circumstances and through the demonstration of this understanding a more realistic and productive contact will ensue.

Social workers occupy a privileged and unique position in relation to people who have legal needs. Here is an opportunity for social workers to assist in enhancing quality of life by sharing their understanding of the law and the legislative framework with clients who may be in crisis and so temporarily unable to make sense of their circumstances, who may be unfamiliar with the legal system, and/or who may be without the necessary social skills to navigate in legal waters. For example, Linda may be unaware of the welfare philosophy underpinning the children's hearing system and so may form expectations more appropriate to a justice model for juvenile offending (emphasising responsibility and retribution), which a social worker would be well placed to discuss with her.

Further opportunities arise for social workers through direct involvement with offenders and ex-offenders. The retention of the probation service functions under the auspices of social work departments has provided the continuing recognition that social work values, knowledge, and skills are most appropriate in dealing with this client population.

Social work law has not yet proved an attractive area of specialisation for solicitors and so there is an additional incentive and requirement for social workers to share their awareness and understanding of the law dimension of their work both with their clients and with other professionals. We are not advocating that social workers become second-rate lawyers but that they use their knowledge of law to inform their practice and contribute to the facilitating of shared social work goals. Martin may deny the grounds of referral, that he stole three pairs of denims from a high street shop, and the social worker would be well placed to explain to Martin and to Linda the process by which the case could now be heard by a sheriff to establish/fail to establish the grounds of referral.

A study of the law relating to social work also contributes to an understanding of the variety of acceptable roles which are appropriate for social workers. In view of society's ambiguous relationship with social workers, these roles are often contradictory and ambivalent. They include investigator, assessor, supervisor, witness, conciliator, reporter, facilitator, liaison, advisor, guide, support, broker, enabler, teacher, mediator, and advocate[1]. Social workers may be in a position to help to identify and enforce the rights of vulnerable clients and/or they may be in the position of enforcing clients' compliance with the law. These roles will be explored in more depth subsequently.

These examples illustrate the importance of a thorough grounding in the relevant law to social work practice. At this point, however, two

1 These last four interventive roles are discussed in B Compton & B Galaway *Social Work Processes* (4th edn) (1989) p 556.

things should be made clear about the operation of law. The first is that law does not necessarily specify a precise course of action to be followed in given circumstances. In most cases there is room for considerable discretion in applying the law, though once it is applied there may be precise procedures to be followed (a good example of this is the law relating to place of safety orders)[1]. The way in which discretion is to be exercised in these areas may be the subject of guidance from the Secretary of State or Social Work Services Group or may be the subject of departmental policies. In such areas knowledge of the guidance and policies is essential, but the underlying legal framework must not be ignored.

Secondly, there are many areas of social work which are not covered specifically or in detail by legislation (eg work with elderly people) and which are simply covered by the general (and very vague) obligation to promote social welfare and assist those in need contained in the Social Work (Scotland) Act 1968 (see below, part 15).

2. THE FUNCTIONS OF LAW IN SOCIETY

Although there has been some dispute about the need for law to regulate society much of that debate is, in fact, about the precise form of law or about its appropriateness as a means of resolving social problems. There is in reality broad agreement about the need for some system of universal rules to regulate the operation of society (the Russian anarchist Kropotkin, for example, noted that 'No society is possible without certain principles of morality generally recognised')[2]. Since social workers' interventions are so inextricably entwined with the functions of law, it is imperative that they understand and appreciate these functions.

The principal functions of law are:

(a) *Social control*. It does this through the enforcement of criminal law and the provision of mechanisms to allow private individuals to resolve their disputes (principally the civil courts). The former of these is often seen, simplistically and erroneously, as the sole or main function of law.

(b) *Constitution of law making and enforcing bodies*. The law also provides for the make up and procedure of Parliament and the court system. As part of this individuals may be given certain

1 See ch 4, pt 3.
2 *Revolutionary Pamphlets*, (1970) p 73.

rights and protections, eg the right of access to legal representation for court appearances.

(c) *Enabling function*. At a very basic level it is sometimes argued that law, by guaranteeing peace, enables people to carry on with their lives. However, it also makes much more specific provision to allow people to make arrangements which will be legally recognised and enforced (eg adoption and contracts).

(d) *Promotion of social welfare*. More recently, particularly since the end of the last world war, law has been used as a tool for the promotion of social welfare. Clearly law cannot do this by itself but rather provides the framework of organisations (eg local authority social work departments) to do so, gives them powers and duties (as it confers these on the employees of social work departments), and confers rights, eg to social security benefits, on individuals.

3. LAW AND SOCIAL PROBLEMS

Social problems are not necessarily amenable to purely legal solutions. For Martin, being obliged to attend a children's hearing may not help him to resolve whatever compelled him to steal. The social worker's involvement with Linda will not necessarily enable her to cope more effectively with the pervasive problems of living for indefinite periods on an inadequate income with few social contacts. However, when the legal solution facilitates the potential resolution of a social problem, as in the example, then the use of such means can be justified.

On a broader level the difficulties of successfully using purely legal means to resolve social problems are illustrated by the failure of anti-discrimination legislation to secure equal pay and employment prospects for women, and the failure, partly as a result of the discretion allowed to local authorities, of the homelessness legislation to cater for those in genuine need of accommodation[1]. In these areas, as in the example we have been looking at, legal intervention has brought about benefits and improvements but, again, on its own is not able to provide a complete resolution of the problem to which it is addressed.

1 See for example the National Audit Office *Homelessness* HC 622 (1989–90) no 622.

4. FORMAL SOURCES OF LAW

Formal sources of law are the actual statements of the law, as opposed to textbooks or commentaries on the law. The main formal sources of law as it affects social workers are Acts of Parliament (statutes); for example – the Social Work (Scotland) Act 1968 (see pt 15 below); delegated legislation – for example, the regulations governing the fostering of children[1]; and case law ie the law derived from decisions made by courts.

As we noted in the previous section, one of the functions of law is the promotion of social welfare, and this has necessitated a fairly substantial volume of legislation. The result of this is that most of the law we will be discussing in the remainder of this book is derived from statute. The precise mechanism for the passing of an Act of Parliament need not concern us here, but it is perhaps worth noting that Acts are often preceded by Green or White Papers or other documents produced by the government setting out its intentions as to legislation. These may allow for comment from interested parties on the proposals before they are finalised. An example of this was in the call for comments to social workers and others concerning the consultation documents for the Child Care Law Review.

For a variety of reasons, for example because of the need for expert professional advice, statutes often omit detailed regulations. The power to make these is usually delegated to a government minister and in the Scottish context this will be the Secretary of State for Scotland. Examples are the rules regulating the conduct of children's hearings and those regulating the use of secure accommodation. Statutes may also provide for the Secretary of State to issue guidance, such as the guidance issued on assumption of parental rights and reviews of children in care. In practice this guidance will come from the Social Work Services Group of the Scottish Office Education Department. The power to make more detailed rules may be delegated to other bodies and an example is the delegation of the power to make procedural rules for civil court cases, as for example to the Court of Session in adoption cases.

One final point of importance on Acts of Parliament is that they do not necessarily or usually become part of the law as soon as they are passed. Instead an Act will usually provide that it is to be brought into force (ie become part of the law) by orders made by the appropriate Secretary of State; a further consequence is that different sections of the Act may be brought into force at different times.

1 See ch 4, pt 7.

Case law may offer a definitive interpretation of the provisions of an Act of Parliament as for example the grounds for assumption of parental rights by the local authority.

Finally regulations and directives made by the European Communities or decisions of the European Court of Justice and the European Court of Human Rights can have an important effect on the law in Scotland.

5. LEGAL PERSONNEL

(1) Solicitors and advocates

The basic division within the legal profession is between solicitors and advocates (the latter are sometimes referred to as counsel). Solicitors are the most numerous. They have direct contact with their clients and may practice in all areas of the law, as is common in smaller towns, or specialise in a particular area of law. The Law Society of Scotland, the solicitor's professional body, publishes a directory of firms indicating the areas of work which they will undertake. The Law Society also acts as the disciplinary body for solicitors. Often social workers develop a local knowledge of solicitors who have a particular interest in social welfare, family law, and/or criminal law which can prove useful to their clients and the Scottish Child Law Centre has compiled a list of solicitors specialising in family and child care law.

Advocates specialise in court appearance and in giving advice on complex matters of law. Historically they had an exclusive right to appear in the higher courts (ie the High Court, Court of Session and House of Lords) but there are now provisions to allow solicitors to appear in these courts. Advocates have no direct contact or relationship with their ultimate client, the relationship is managed by the client's solicitors.

(2) Procurators fiscal

Scotland has always operated a system of public prosecution where prosecutions are undertaken by a body independent from the police. This system of public prosecution is headed by the Lord Advocate, a political appointee. He is assisted by the Solicitor General (these two are the Law Officers), again a political appointee, and a number of Advocates-Depute. This permanent service operates from the Crown Office in Edinburgh which is headed by the Crown Agent; procurators fiscal are the local representatives of this service. Normally each sheriff court district will have a procurator fiscal who will be assisted by a number of procurators fiscal depute (the procurator fiscal and procurators fiscal depute are usually simply referred to as fiscals).

Reports of crime are made by the police to the fiscal who will then, in theory, direct any further investigation. In practice in most cases no further investigation is necessary or takes place.

In summary cases (for an explanation of this see below) the whole power of decision as to whether or not to prosecute and which court to prosecute in – district or sheriff – is in the hands of the fiscal. The fiscal is, however, subject to certain statutory restrictions (which may provide that a crime cannot be tried in the district court) and operates under general guidelines issued by the Crown Office.

In cases where solemn procedure (again see below) is contemplated a report is made to the Crown Office for their instructions as to how to proceed.

Prosecutions in the sheriff and district courts will be undertaken by the fiscal or a depute. In the High Court the prosecutor will be one of the Law Officers or an Advocate Depute.

In cases where there is sufficient evidence to proceed to prosecution the fiscal may, instead of prosecuting, administer a warning. Before this can be done there must be sufficient evidence to justify proceedings and the case must not be so trivial as to merit no action. Fiscals also have the power in certain types of cases to offer an individual the option of paying a fixed penalty as an alternative to prosecution. Finally, there are a number of diversion schemes in operation where individuals are diverted to social work assistance in place of prosecution. Diversion schemes and procurator fiscal fines are both considered in chapter 6, part 5.

As well as being a prosecutor the fiscal is also responsible for investigating all sudden and suspicious deaths and suicides.

(3) Judges

District courts are most often presided over by one or more lay magistrates. These are people who have no legal training but have been appointed to act as magistrates. They will be guided as to the law by a legal assessor or by the clerk to the court. The practice as to the number of magistrates sitting to hear a case and the source of legal guidance varies between different areas. There are also, in Glasgow District Court, a number of stipendiary magistrates. These magistrates are legally qualified and sit alone to hear cases. They have greater sentencing powers than lay magistrates.

Sheriff courts are staffed by sheriffs who are legally qualified, most having been advocates.

Finally there are the judges who preside both in the Court of Session and High Court. They are all legally qualified and are variously described as Lords of Session, Lord Commissioners of Justiciary and Senators of the College of Justice. How they are described depends on which role they are fulfilling.

(4) Clerks of court

The most numerous of these are sheriff clerks. They are responsible for the running of sheriff courts, recording of proceedings (though not shorthand note-taking), arranging for reports, arranging (in consultation with the procurator fiscal) the court timetable, maintenance of records, collection of fines, and the organisation and distribution of social enquiry reports. This last task will involve co-operation with the social worker(s) attached to the court, who will make arrangements with the appropriate social work area office for the report to be provided. Each sheriff court will have a sheriff-clerk who will be assisted by deputes.

The district and High Courts have clerks who broadly perform the same function for them as sheriff clerks do for the sheriff court.

(5) Sheriff officers

These are officers of court who must fulfil certain requirements and hold a warrant from the sheriff to act. They are not directly employed by the court system but rather are court officers in the sense that they are authorised to do certain things by virtue of their warrant and are accountable to court for their actions. Sheriff officers are used to serve summonses and citations in civil cases, to carry out the enforcement of civil judgements eg evictions and warrant sales, and to serve witness citations for the defence in criminal cases.

(6) Miscellaneous

As well as those noted above there are a variety of other people involved in the operation of the court system. These include ushers and bar officers who assist in the actual functioning of the courts, directing people to the right court and maintaining order in court.

6. CIVIL COURT SYSTEM

The civil court system basically deals with all cases which do not involve the commission of a crime or offence and which are not dealt with by a special body, eg an industrial tribunal. Examples of the sorts of case it deals with are given below. Before going on to look at the various courts in the civil court system some explanation of the distinction between courts of first instance and courts of appeal is necessary. Courts of first instance are the courts where a case appears and is dealt with, ie these are the courts at which trials take place and in which civil cases are disposed. Appeal courts deal only or mainly with appeals from the decisions of courts of first instance.

(1) Sheriff court

Scotland is divided up into six sheriffdoms, five of these (the exception being Glasgow and Strathkelvin) are then subdivided into sheriff court districts, each of which has a sheriff court building. Each sheriffdom is staffed by a sheriff principal and a number of sheriffs. The precise organisation of the court will depend on the level of business; in rural areas, for example, the court may only sit on one day a week or as necessary to deal with the business.

The sheriff civil court involves a sheriff sitting alone to deal with cases at first instance. It cannot deal with some matters; the main exclusions being legitimacy, setting aside of documents and judicial review (see below, part 13). On the other hand there are certain matters that can only be dealt with at the sheriff court, eg eviction and actions for sums of money less than £1,500.

The sheriff civil court deals with such matters as adoption, proofs on reference from children's hearings, divorce, applications under the Mental Health (Scotland) Act 1984 and (accounting for most of its business) small debt actions.

Decisions of the sheriff can be appealed to the sheriff principal or direct to the Inner House of the Court of Session.

(2) Court of Session

The Court of Session sits only in Edinburgh. It is divided into an Outer House which consists of judges sitting alone to deal with cases at first instance and an Inner House. The Inner House is divided into two divisions of four judges (though only three usually sit in a case) and deals primarily with appeals from the Outer House and from the sheriff court and sheriff principal. The Inner House is also a court of first instance for a variety of applications under companies legislation and other specialised forms of procedure. Appeals involving the assumption of parental rights and arising from the children's hearing system may end up in the Inner House.

(3) House of Lords

This operates only as a court of appeal. In cases originating in the sheriff court the appeal must be concerned with a question of law rather than a factual dispute.

7. CRIMINAL COURT SYSTEM[1]

Within the criminal court system there is a distinction between solemn and summary courts. The essential distinction between these is that in summary courts the judge(s) takes the decision on guilt or innocence, whereas in solemn courts this is done by a jury of 15. There are also some differences in the procedure followed in the different types of court, these will be considered more fully below.

(1) District court

District courts are based on local authority districts, and local authorities have certain responsibilities in relation to provision of accommodation and staffing. As noted above the district court will normally be presided over by a lay magistrate or lay magistrates with legal advice from an assessor or clerk of court.

The sorts of cases the district court can deal with are restricted. It cannot deal with housebreaking cases, serious assaults, forgery, theft and fraud cases where the amount involved is more than £2,500, and cases involving the prosecution of children under 16.

The sentencing powers of the court are limited to a fine of up to Level 4 (currently £2,500)[2] and up to 60 days imprisonment. Where the court is presided over by a stipendiary magistrate it has the same sentencing powers as the sheriff summary court. As always in this chapter references to sentencing powers are to the maximum sentence that can be imposed in the absence of a specific statutory provision

1 See also ch 6, pts 3, 4 and 7.
2 See ch 6, pt 4(4).

restricting or enhancing the power in respect of particular crimes or offences.

Currently the district court deals with about half of criminal cases.

(2) Sheriff summary court

The sheriff summary court is held in the same buildings and staffed by the same personnel as the sheriff civil court.

The sentencing powers of this court are, currently, a fine of £5,000 and three months imprisonment. In cases where the person being sentenced has committed a crime of violence or of dishonesty and he/she has a previous conviction for a crime of violence in the former case or dishonesty in the latter case the maximum possible period of imprisonment is six months.

The sheriff summary court deals with about half of all criminal cases.

(3) Sheriff solemn court

The sheriff solemn court deals with slightly more serious cases and this is reflected in its sentencing power. The sheriff sitting in this court can impose an unlimited fine and imprison for up to three years. In cases where the sheriff considers that these sentencing powers are inadequate the case can be remitted to the High Court for sentence. This happens very rarely in practice.

The sheriff solemn court deals with about 1% of criminal cases.

(4) High Court of Justiciary

Although this has the same personnel as the Court of Session it sits not only in Edinburgh but also at locations throughout Scotland, and is, for example, in almost permanent session in Glasgow. The High Court is the only court which can deal with certain crimes, the most notable being murder and rape.

The High Court deals with about 1% of criminal cases.

(5) High Court as court of appeal

The High Court has always operated as a court of appeal from summary courts. For this purpose it sits in Edinburgh and is presided over by three judges. Since 1926 it has also operated in the same format as the Court of Criminal Appeal to deal with appeals from solemn courts.

8. EUROPEAN COURTS

(1) European Court of Justice

The European Court of Justice is the court of the European Communities and is responsible for the interpretation of European Community legislation. This interpretation is authoritative and affects the law in member states. The court has made a number of significant decisions regarding equal pay and equal rights at work.

(2) European Court of Human Rights

The United Kingdom is a signatory to the European Convention on Human Rights and has accepted the jurisdiction of the Court in disputes under the Convention. The procedure for making and deciding on an application is complex and time consuming. Britain has been found guilty of breaches of the Convention on a number of occasions in cases concerning, for example, the censoring of prisoners' mail and the rights of parents of children in care.

9. CIVIL PROCEDURE[1]

(1) Small claims procedure

This type of procedure was introduced in 1988 and is designed to provide a simple and inexpensive form of action which can be easily used by members of the public. It can be used to recover money up to £750 or for the recovery of property up to that value. Most cases in practice are of the former type and may be actions to recover debts (most commonly) or actions to recover damages.

There is no provision for legal aid in this process (see below) as the intention is that private individuals will be able to conduct cases themselves. There is, however, provision allowing either party to be represented at any hearing by any other person. Where that person is not a solicitor the sheriff must be satisfied that he/she is a 'suitable person'.

1 See also ch 2, pt 4.

(2) Summary cause procedure

Summary cause procedure, again a simplified form of procedure, is similar to small claims procedure. It is the appropriate means of recovering sums of money between £750 and £1,500; it is also used for actions for eviction[1].

(3) Ordinary procedure

This form of procedure is used in the sheriff court. It is appropriate for claims in excess of £1,500 and for other types of case, including divorces not covered by the 'do-it-yourself' procedure[2]. Procedure in the Court of Session is similar to this. Unlike small claims and summary cause procedure, this type of procedure is based on extensive written pleadings (essentially the claims and counter-claims made by the parties to the court action). This makes it too complex and unsuitable for claims involving small amounts and also means that considerable delays are built into the process.

(4) Special procedures

A variety of types of case of interest to social workers have their own special forms of procedure. These include proof of grounds of referral to a children's hearing, appeals from hearing decisions and adoption. The procedures will be explained in more detail when we look at these areas.

(5) Standard of proof

The standard of proof in civil cases is proof on the balance of probabilities. Generally, then, the person initiating the case must satisfy the court that his/her version of events is more probable than that put forward by the other party.

10. CRIMINAL PROCEDURE

(1) Summary procedure

Summary procedure is initiated by the service of a document known as a complaint on the accused. The complaint will contain brief details

1 See also ch 2, pt 2.
2 See ch 3, pt 3.

of the alleged offence including the time and date. Attached to the complaint will be a notice of previous convictions, if relevant, and in the case of statutory offences a notice of penalties setting out the possible penalties on conviction.

On the first appearance of the accused, either from custody or on the date specified for the hearing on the citation accompanying the complaint, the plea will be taken. This diet is, for this reason, sometimes referred to as the pleading diet. If the accused pleads guilty the court may proceed to sentence, or may defer sentence (D/S) for reports or for the accused to be of good behaviour. If the accused pleads not guilty a date will be set for trial.

If the accused pleads not guilty there may be an intermediate diet called before the trial diet. The purpose of this diet is to assess the state of preparation on both sides and the accused's intentions as to plea. The reason for introducing this intermediate diet was the common practice of pleading not guilty at the first diet and changing the plea to guilty at the trial. It has not been much used in practice.

Procedure at the trial is considered on page 15.

(2) Solemn procedure

The accused's first appearance will be on petition. The petition will specify the preliminary form of the charge against him/her. This first hearing will take the form of a judicial examination in front of the sheriff in the sheriff's chambers. The fiscal may ask questions at this stage and a transcript of the questions and any answers may be read out at any subsequent trial. After examination the accused may be committed for further examination, in which case he/she will appear before the sheriff again, or may be committed for trial (sometimes described as being fully committed), and may be released on bail or kept in custody.

Once the accused has been committed for trial an indictment will be served on him/her (assuming that the case is proceeding). The indictment will contain the final version of the charge against the accused, will specify a date for the trial and will have attached to it, as appropriate, a notice of previous convictions, as well as a list of the prosecution witnesses and of any productions (ie any physical evidence such as photographs or weapons) the prosecution intend to present at the trial.

If the accused is kept in custody the indictment must be served within 80 days and the trial start within 110 days, in both cases starting with the date of full committal. If the accused is at liberty the trial must start within 12 months of the first appearance on petition.

SUMMARY PROCEDURE (Appearance from custody)

Pleading Diet —— Guilty —— Sentence or D/S

(Duty solicitor available)

Not guilty

Trial date set

May be remanded in custody or liberated pending trial

Application for legal aid

Trial diet —— Not guilty —— Released

Guilty

Sentence or D/S

Where the appearance is not from custody the duty solicitor is not available to assist at the pleading diet[1].

1 See pt 14 below on legal aid.

SOLEMN PROCEDURE

Appearance on petition (ie judicial examination in sheriff court)

continued for further examination

Committal for trial

Bail or custody

Service of indictment (note time limits)

Trial diet (at sheriff or High Court)

(3) Procedure at trial

Over 90% of criminal cases do not go to trial, the accused simply pleads guilty and is sentenced. Although the accused has a right to defend him/herself in those cases that go to trial legal representation can greatly assist the accused's case and make sure it is properly presented.

Procedure at trial is similar in both solemn and summary procedure, the main differences being due to the presence of the jury in solemn procedure. The main stages are:

(a) Presentation of the prosecution evidence. There are no opening statements in Scottish trials of the sort which might be familiar from American films or television. The prosecution simply call their first witness and the trial proceeds from there. Each witness will be examined by the prosecution (this initial questioning is known as the examination in chief), he/she will then be cross-examined by the defence and then, if necessary, be re-examined by the prosecution.

(b) At the end of the prosecution case the defence may move that the charges be dropped on the ground that there is no case to answer, in other words that the prosecution has not produced sufficient evidence to find the accused guilty.

(c) If this motion is rejected the defence will then present their evidence in the same way as the prosecution. There is, of course, no need for the defence to give evidence, or, more particularly, for the accused to give evidence, though this may be commented on by the judge. It is up to the prosecution to prove their case beyond reasonable doubt.

(d) Following the defence case both sides, prosecution first, will make their concluding speeches. In summary cases these are addressed to the judge(s), in solemn cases to the jury.

(e) In solemn cases the judge will then address the jury explaining their function, the standard of proof which the prosecution must meet and any relevant legal points. The judge will usually also highlight some of the significant points of evidence, although the jurors must decide on their own recollection of the evidence. After this the jury will retire to consider its verdict, a process which is widely recognised to be far from scientific.

(f) The judge or jury will then reach a verdict. The verdict may be guilty, not guilty or not proven. This last is a Scottish curiosity and appears to mean 'we rather suspect that you are guilty, but the evidence has not persuaded us beyond a reasonable doubt'.

(g) Following a guilty verdict the court will move on to sentence. In solemn cases the prosecution must move for sentence to be passed, otherwise the judge cannot pass sentence. Sentence may be deferred either for reports or for some other reason, for example, for the accused to show that he/she can be of good behaviour or for repayment of a sum of money dishonestly obtained. In some cases the judge must obtain social enquiry reports before sentencing, for example, when considering a custodial disposal for an offender not previously sentenced to custody or for an offender under 21. Before sentence is passed the accused's solicitor or counsel will normally make a plea in mitigation, the purpose of which is to attempt to influence the sentencer to be lenient.

(4) Standard of proof

As we have noted the standard of proof in criminal cases is proof beyond reasonable doubt. This is more exacting than the standard in civil cases and requires the prosecution to produce evidence which does not leave any reasonable doubt in the mind of the judge (in summary cases) or the jury (in solemn cases) as to the guilt of the accused. This standard of proof is also relevant in hearings before the sheriff to establish a referral to a children's hearing on offence grounds[1].

(5) Bail

Bail may be applied for on any appearance in court and refusal of bail can be appealed against except where it takes place in solemn proceedings prior to full committal. The only non-bailable offences are murder and treason. An individual may be released on bail both before conviction and after conviction but before sentence, he/she may also be released pending the outcome of an appeal against a custodial sentence.

In deciding on whether to grant bail the court must consider the public interest and the possibility of intimidation of witnesses. If bail is granted the person released on bail will be subject to a number of conditions set out in the Bail (Scotland) Act 1980. These are:

(a) He/she must appear at all court diets.
(b) He/she must not commit further offences.
(c) He/she must not interfere with witnesses.
(d) He/she must make him/herself available for the purposes of enabling enquiries or reports to be made to assist the courts disposition of the case. This would include, for example, a social enquiry report requested by a court prior to sentencing.

The court may attach other conditions to the granting of bail as appropriate. Generally speaking, lodging of a sum of money in court by way of guaranteeing future appearances is not required unless there are special circumstances.

It is important to note that breach of any of the bail conditions is itself a criminal offence. So, for example, if a person on bail refused to co-operate with a social worker in the compilation of a social enquiry

1 See ch 4, pt 4(6).

report he/she would be breaching one of the conditions of bail and committing a further offence.

(6) Appeals

Appeals can be made against both conviction and sentence. If the appeal is against sentence it must be shown to be unreasonable. There is a slight disincentive to appealing against sentence in that the court can increase as well as decrease the sentence on appeal.

(7) Accelerated diets

There is provision for accelerated diets to take place. This would happen when an accused who has pled not guilty changes his/her plea to guilty, sometimes after some negotiation of the charges with the prosecution, and wishes the matter dealt with before the date set for the trial diet. In solemn procedure this is known as section 102 procedure.

11. CHILDREN'S HEARINGS

The system of children's hearings was introduced by the Social Work (Scotland) Act 1968 to deal with a whole range of cases relating to children which were formerly dealt with in a variety of different courts. These include offences committed by children, children beyond parental control, children against whom offences may have been committed and children who truant. Children's hearings are considered in greater detail in chapter 4, part 4.

12. ADMINISTRATIVE TRIBUNALS

Administrative tribunals have been set up to adjudicate in a wide variety of areas affected by state intervention. Examples are social security appeal tribunals, rent assessment committees and industrial tribunals. Procedure and the rules of representation before tribunals are generally much more relaxed than those before courts. This opens up greater possibilities for the representation, for example, of claimants before social security appeals tribunals. This is particularly important as there is evidence to suggest that claimants who are represented have a greater chance of success than those who are not.

Welfare rights officers and social workers are sometimes found representing claimants.

13. JUDICIAL REVIEW

Judicial review is a procedure by which decisions of many public bodies may be challenged. It differs from appeal in that the right to seek review exists without the express statutory provision which is needed to create a right of appeal; indeed the courts have sometimes reviewed decisions in spite of specific statutory provisions excluding their jurisdiction. This makes review particularly useful in cases where there is no provision for appeal against a decision.

There are, however, two major drawbacks to using judicial review to challenge decisions. The first of these is that actions for judicial review can only be dealt with by the Court of Session in Edinburgh. This is not as much of a problem as it used to be following the introduction of a simpler and quicker form of procedure, though it makes the process more expensive than it would otherwise be. The second drawback is that review can only be sought on restricted grounds. To succeed the applicant must be able to show that the person or body taking the decision acted outwith their powers, acted unreasonably, or did not comply with the requirements of natural justice.

Despite these drawbacks judicial review has been a valuable remedy in certain areas. The most prominent in recent years has been its use by people who have been refused accommodation under the homelessness legislation, made necessary because there is no statutory provision for appeal against a local authority decision to refuse housing. One example is the case of *Kelly v Monklands District Council*[1]. In this case a 16-year-old girl left home because of violence by her father against her. She had nowhere to stay and had attempted suicide. She applied for housing as a homeless person. One of the cases in which an authority is bound to provide housing is if the applicant is vulnerable. The local authority decided that Ms Kelly was not vulnerable despite a report from the social work department to the contrary. The court decided that the authority had acted unreasonably in arriving at their conclusion on vulnerability and in not taking proper account of the report from the social work department. The council was ordered to house Ms Kelly[2].

1 1986 SLT 169.
2 See also ch 2, pt 2(3).

14. LEGAL AID

Legal aid in Scotland is administered by the Scottish Legal Aid Board. There are three types of legal aid: legal advice and assistance; civil legal aid; and criminal legal aid.

(1) Legal advice and assistance

This is a means tested scheme which provides free advice and assistance to applicants who qualify on the basis of a means test. Above the qualifying level for free assistance there is a sliding scale for contribution up to the point where full payment must be made. People in receipt of income support or family credit qualify automatically on income grounds, but may be ineligible through their ownership of capital above the permitted limit. The decision as to entitlement is made by the solicitor who is approached for advice.

Legal advice and assistance covers advice about any matter of Scots law and, with very limited exceptions, only covers assistance short of representation before a court or tribunal. One exception is appeals under the Mental Health (Scotland) Act 1984[1].

(2) Civil legal aid

Civil legal aid is available to raise or defend actions in the civil courts. Once again it is means tested, and again those in receipt of income support or family credit will qualify automatically on income grounds. As with legal advice and assistance there is a sliding scale of contributions above the level of free entitlement, up to the point where the applicant is not entitled to any assistance.

This is the type of legal aid that would be appropriate for action, for example under the Social Work (Scotland) Act 1968 and with regard to adoptions.

In urgent cases emergency legal aid can be obtained immediately. This might be necessary, for example, to allow a woman to obtain an interim exclusion order excluding a violent spouse from the family home[2].

1 See ch 5, pt 4.
2 See ch 3, pt 4.

(3) Criminal legal aid

The operation of this scheme depends on whether or not the first appearance in court is made from custody and whether the prosecution is solemn or summary. Applications for legal aid in solemn cases are decided by the court while applications in summary cases go to the Board. The granting of legal aid is almost automatic in solemn cases. The only ground for refusal is that the accused could pay for his/her defence without undue hardship. Where an accused appears in court from custody he/she is entitled to be represented by the duty solicitor assigned to that court.

15. THE SOCIAL WORK (SCOTLAND) ACT 1968

(1) Introduction

The Social Work (Scotland) Act 1968 grew out of two developments. The first was a trend towards generic social work based on the view that social work with all types of people has a common base of values and skills. The second was the recommendation of the Kilbrandon Report[1] for the setting up of a social education department to provide support for the children's hearings which they proposed. These two developments were brought together in the White Paper *Social Work and the Community*[2] which formed the basis for the 1968 Act.

The 1968 Act is one of the core pieces of legislation, providing much of the framework for the activities of social workers employed by local authorities, as well as setting down specific duties and specific procedures that have to be followed in particular circumstances. For that reason it is worth undertaking a brief survey of the Act at this point. Parts of it will be dealt with in more detail later in the book.

The major contribution of the 1968 Act, as far as provision of social work services is concerned, was to draw all of the disparate services provided by local authorities into one department under one overall director and with a council committee responsible for its oversight.

(2) Persons in need and assessments

In keeping with the interventionist tenor of the times, section 12 of the 1968 Act imposes an overall duty to 'promote social welfare' by

1 *Children and Young Persons* Cmnd 2306 (1964).
2 Cmnd 3065(1966).

making available advice, guidance and assistance and securing the provision of facilities, including residential accommodation.

This section also allows the provision of assistance in cash or kind in certain circumstances. Firstly, such assistance can be provided where it would be likely to diminish the need (a) to receive a child into care or keep him/her in care, or (b) of a child being referred to a children's hearing. Secondly, this type of assistance can be provided to a 'person in need' (see below) where doing so would avoid greater cost to the local authority either in the provision of some other service, eg the direct provision of accommodation, or at some future date. In this second category of cases cash assistance can only be given in an emergency. Social work departments have their own policies and practices in relation to the giving of section 12 assistance. It should be noted that it is not intended to operate as an alternative to the benefits system and that assistance can be made conditional on repayment.

Various interpretations in different authorities and within authorities have led to enormous variation in the use of section 12. Strategies which have encompassed the promotional use of these funds and those which have used the funds for preventative services have come and gone over the years. Decisions to limit the interpretation and penalise authorities who acted otherwise, as in the policy of Strathclyde Regional Council social work department to use section 12 funds to support single striking miners, have influenced more recent understandings of the use of section 12 funds. The bureaucratic hierarchical structures of social work departments have also been reflected in the policies of departments regarding the amounts of section 12 money which can be dispensed to the public by various grades of staff. For example, many basic grade social workers can only dispense £10 without authorisation from a higher grade member of staff.

Section 14 deals with the provision of domiciliary services (usually referred to as home helps) for households including a person in need or expectant mother, and also the provision of laundry services in such cases. These services are provided directly by the local authority.

As we have seen these provisions refer to persons in need, defined in the Act as being persons who:

(a) are in need of care and attention arising out of infirmity, youth or age; or
(b) suffer from illness or mental disorder or are substantially handicapped by any deformity or disability; or
(c) being persons prescribed by the Secretary of State who have asked for assistance, are, in the opinion of a local authority, persons to

whom the local authority may appropriately make available the services and facilities provided by them under the 1968 Act[1].

In addition, for the purposes of section 12 only, the definition is extended to include those in need as a result of drug or alcohol dependence and release from prison or other form of detention[2].

Section 12A of the Act, added by the National Health Service and Community Care Act 1990, requires the authority to carry out an assessment of need before providing 'community care services'. This provision, which takes effect from 1 April 1993, is considered more fully in chapter 5, part 2.

(3) Children in need

The Act imposes an obligation to take into care children who are in need, basically children whose parents are unable to care for them. Chapter 4, part 2 considers these provisions in more detail.

(4) Children's hearings and compulsory care

Part III of the Act sets up the system of children's hearings which was recommended by the Kilbrandon Report. It sets out the grounds for referral, procedures and the duties of the social work department. These provisions are considered more fully in chapter 4, part 4.

(5) Reports and supervision of offenders

Section 27 deals with the responsibilities of the social work department in relation to the provision of reports to criminal courts and the provision of supervision to probationers and those released from custody on licence. Chapter 6, parts 2, 4 and 8, looks at this area in more detail.

(6) Residential establishments

Part IV of the Act deals with the provision of residential establishments by local authorities and provides a system for registration of other residential establishments, for example private residential homes for persons who are elderly, with the local authority.

1 Section 94(1), the Secretary of State has not made use of the power given here.
2 Section 12(6).

(7) Complaints procedure

Since 1 April 1991 local authorities must have a complaints procedure to deal with representations (including complaints) about the authority's performance, or lack of performance, of their obligations under the 1968 Act and various other pieces of legislation (eg the Disabled Persons (Services, Consultation and Representation) Act 1986). There is no national representations procedure, rather each authority will have developed its own.

16. THE CHILDREN ACT 1989

This piece of legislation, which made fundamental changes to child care law in England and Wales has little application in Scotland. Apart from some minor amendments there are three provisions it is worth noting. Firstly, the Act imposes a duty on local authorities to review the provision of day care for the under eights. Secondly, a scheme of registration for child minders and those providing day care services for under eights is introduced. The responsibility for running this registration scheme rests with the social work department. Thirdly, the Act amends adoption law to provide that the if the father/mother of the child being adopted is one of the adoptive parents he/she need only be 18 at the date of adoption, provided his/her partner is 21[1].

1 See ch 3, pt 3.

2. General law relevant to social work

1. INTRODUCTION

As well as a knowledge of what has been described as professional law, ie that law which is central to the professional activities of a social worker, social workers also need to have some knowledge of other areas of law in order to be able to assist clients with some of the problems and concerns they may have. This chapter is intended to give a brief outline of the law in the areas of housing, welfare benefits, discrimination, debt, access to information and education. The coverage is not exhaustive and we have attempted to give further references where more detail may be found. It may also be the case that where a client has a problem in these areas he/she would be well advised to seek qualified legal advice, perhaps under the Legal Advice and Assistance Scheme.

2. HOUSING

(1) Rights to repair

Certain obligations are imposed on all landlords whether in the private or public sector in respect of repairs to premises. In this context the public sector consists mainly of houses let by local authorities, Scottish Homes and development corporations. Houses let by housing associations are now regarded as being in the private sector, at least as far as most legislation is concerned.

There is a general common law duty to keep premises wind and water tight and in a proper tenantable condition. An example of breach of this duty is *McArdle v Glasgow District Council*[1] where a tenant successfully sued the landlord for damages as a result of chronic dampness in the flat.

1 1989 SCLR 19.

There are also a number of statutory obligations imposed on landlords:

(a) Properties let for a rent of less than £300 per week (ie most properties) must be in all respects fit for human habitation at the start of the tenancy and must be maintained by the landlord in that condition. In deciding whether the property is fit for human habitation consideration is given to the extent to which the house falls short of the requirements of the building regulations.
(b) For properties let for less than seven years the landlord must keep the structure and exterior of the house in good repair and inside the house must keep the gas, water and electricity supply, the sanitary appliances, and space and water heaters in good repair and working properly. The restriction on the length of tenancies has little practical effect as most tenancies, including those in the public sector, are for less than seven years.
(c) Where the landlord is responsible for the maintenance and repair of the premises he/she must take reasonable care in carrying out this responsibility so as to prevent danger to people coming into the premises. *Hughes Tutrix v Glasgow District Council*[1] is an example where a mother successfully sued for damages for her daughter who was injured on a defective toilet bowl.

In addition to the statutory and common law responsibilities other obligations may be imposed on the landlord in the lease of the property.

If the landlord fails in carrying out these obligations the tenant has a number of remedies. He/she may, unless this is excluded by the lease, withhold his/her rent or take legal action against the landlord for damages or for an order requiring the landlord to meet his/her obligations. Where the tenant withholds rent all of the arrears of rent must be repaid when the landlord fixes the defect.

District and islands councils also have power to take action against properties which are in disrepair or which are dangerous to health. They may, of course, be reluctant to use these powers where they own the property.

Social workers have no mandatory duties in relation to people whose assessed needs relate to the completion of housing repairs other than under the pervasive umbrella of the duty to promote social welfare contained in section 12 of the Social Work (Scotland) Act 1968. However a social worker may be well placed to advise the client

1 1982 SLT (Sh Ct) 7O.

what legal obligations fall to the landlord and what remedies fall to the tenant.

Using the legal knowledge available to inform social work practice can contribute to the empowerment of the client in arranging, for example, for repairs to be completed. It may well be agreed that the social worker becomes actively involved taking on the role of liaison or advocate with the housing authority, while continuing to support the client through what may well be experienced as a very stressful experience.

(2) **Eviction**

Generally tenants cannot be removed from a property until the landlord has obtained an order for recovery of possession of the property from the sheriff court. Before any landlord can commence court proceedings to obtain such an order for recovery of possession of property he/she must serve a notice to quit or, in public sector tenancies, a notice of intention to start proceedings on the tenant. This applies to all tenancies, whether or not they enjoy some other form of statutory protection (see below) and must give the tenant at least 28 days notice. In addition, where the tenant enjoys some form of statutory protection, the notice to quit must contain certain specified information including advice to the tenant on possible sources of information and assistance. If the notice to quit does not contain this information it is invalid, and the landlord cannot rely on it in proceedings for recovery of possession. For assured tenancies (basically private sector tenancies starting after January 1989) the notice to quit must be accompanied by a notice of intention to raise an action for possession.

Tenancies enjoying statutory protection include nearly all public sector tenancies as well as most in the private sector. The main exceptions are premises with a resident landlord and tenancies where the landlord is an educational institution. In this context it is perhaps worth noting that housing association tenants enjoy protection as public sector tenants if their tenancy started before January 1989; tenants with tenancies starting after that date are protected as assured tenants.

Where a tenant does enjoy some form of statutory protection the effect of this is that the court will only grant an order for possession on certain restricted grounds eg non-payment of rent or causing a nuisance to neighbours.

Finally, in many cases the sheriff has the power to adjourn the hearing. This power might be used, for example, to allow payment of arrears of rent or to allow a 'bad neighbour' to mend his/her ways.

Social workers should help the client identify what type of tenancy he/she has. This will of course influence which set of statutory procedures and protections apply. The process of possible eviction is potentially extremely stressful and if a social worker is involved with the person/family threatened with eviction there are a number of things which may prove helpful in diminishing unnecessary stress. For example, it may help the person/family to learn that the notice means that there are at least 28 days before the council (or other landlord) can apply to the sheriff for an order for recovery of possession (an eviction order) and that they cannot be removed until there has been a hearing and the sheriff has issued such an order. If the notice to quit is not in the statutory form designed for this purpose, then the client may be helped by learning that it is invalid.

So, the social worker should advise the client not to leave their home unless they already have alternative accommodation and want to leave, to get legal advice under the legal advice and assistance scheme[1], to attend the court hearing and/or arrange for an application to be made to the court on their behalf. Tenants who attend the hearing or are represented at the hearing are less likely to be evicted.

The social worker may determine that it would be appropriate to negotiate with the client to act as an advocate on their behalf to the housing authority or the sheriff court. The client may require the social worker to act as liaison with other agencies for a limited period until their level of coping has been restored.

(3) Homelessness

Homelessness is a growing problem both in Britain as a whole and in Scotland. There are a variety of reasons for this, including the decline in the private rented sector and the decline in the number of public sector houses available for rent. The number of young people leaving local authority care who become homeless should be of particular concern to social workers[2].

Until 1977 the duty to provide for those who became homeless rested on social work departments. In 1977 the Housing (Homeless Persons) Act was passed and this transferred the responsibility to housing authorities. It came into effect in Scotland on 1 April 1978. The law is now contained in Part II of the Housing (Scotland) Act 1987 which operates in conjunction with a code of guidance issued to local authorities by the Secretary of State in 1991.

1 See ch 1, pt 14.
2 For an overview see J Greve *Homelessness in Britain* (1991).

When someone approaches a housing authority for assistance the first obligation on the authority is to carry out initial inquiries. These may involve a request for information from the social work department. The code of guidance suggests that the investigation should be completed in 30 days. The inquiries are directed towards answering three questions:

(a) Is the applicant homeless or threatened with homelessness?
(b) Is the applicant in this position intentionally?
(c) Does the applicant have priority need?

While these inquiries are being carried out and if the authority have reason to believe that the applicant is homeless and has priority need the authority must provide temporary accommodation pending the completion of the inquiries.

(a) Is the applicant homeless or threatened with homelessness?

A person is homeless for the purpose of the Act if **either**:

(i) There is no accommodation which he/she is legally entitled to occupy (eg as a tenant or owner/occupier). The accommodation must be such that the applicant could reasonably occupy it together with any member of his/her family normally living with them. Thus families living in separate accommodation will be regarded as homeless as will those living in temporary accommodation. A person is not to be regarded as having accommodation unless it would be reasonable for him/her to continue to occupy it;
(ii) accommodation is available to him/her but either:
  - he/she cannot secure entry to the property; or
  - occupying the accommodation will lead to violence or threats of violence which are likely to be carried out by someone else residing in the accommodation; or
  - occupying the property will probably lead to violence, or threats of violence which are likely to be carried out, from someone who previously shared accommodation with him/her; or
  - the accommodation is a houseboat or mobile home but there is no mooring or pitching place available; or
  - it is overcrowded as defined in the Housing (Scotland) Act 1987[1]

1 Sections 135–7. This consists of a room standard which is contravened if two people of opposite sexes over ten who are not married have to share accommodation and a space standard which provides, for example, that a three room house is overcrowded if more than five people over ten live there.

and may endanger the health of the occupants. Note that both parts of this requirement must be fulfilled.

The provision that a person can be treated as homeless if it is not reasonable for him/her to continue staying in their present accommodation can cover a number of circumstances which are not specifically provided for. Examples are cases where he/she is subjected to violence or threats from neighbours, or the accommodation is overcrowded but not dangerous to health.

A person is threatened with homelessness if he/she is likely to become homeless within the next 28 days.

(*b*) *Is the applicant in this position intentionally?*

The applicant will be regarded as intentionally homeless if he/she deliberately does or fails to do something which results in him/her no longer occupying accommodation which was available. It must also have been reasonable to expect the applicant to continue staying in the accommodation he/she has left.

In this context a deliberate act or omission is one which is intentional and which would lead a reasonable person to expect eviction as a result of it. It does not apply to anything done in good faith or in ignorance of any relevant fact. The case of *Wincentzen v Monklands District Council*[1] illustrates this. In this case a young woman left home temporarily despite her father's warning, which she did not believe, that she would not be allowed to return. When she returned her father refused her access to the house. The Court of Session decided that she was not intentionally homeless as when she left she had acted in good faith and in ignorance of the relevant fact that her father meant what he said. There must be a clear causal link between the act or omission and the homelessness.

In determining whether it is reasonable for the applicant to have stayed in the accommodation the authority should consider not only the condition of the property but also the applicant's reasons for leaving and personal circumstances. The code of guidance suggests, for example, that severe emotional stress would be an acceptable reason for leaving accommodation.

The same considerations are relevant in deciding whether someone is intentionally threatened with homelessness. Examples of intentional homelessness would include eviction due to non-payment of rent and voluntarily leaving accommodation which was still available and

1 1988 SLT 259.

which it was reasonable to continue to occupy. In the former case, however, the code of guidance suggests that where rent arrears were due to real personal or financial difficulties the applicant should not be regarded as intentionally homeless.

Once someone has been found to be intentionally homeless this is not a finding which lasts for all time, and it should be reviewed as circumstances change.

(c) Does the applicant have priority need?

There are four categories of applicant with priority need:

(i) Those who have dependent children, ie, children under the age of 16 or those under the age of 19 undergoing full-time education or training or who are unable to support themselves. The children must either be residing with the applicant or it must be reasonable to expect them to reside together. This last proviso ensures that families split up in temporary accommodation will not therefore be deprived of priority status.

(ii) Those whose homelessness or threatened homelessness is due to an emergency such as flood, fire or another disaster.

(iii) Those who are or have somebody who might be expected to live with them who is vulnerable as a result of old age, mental illness or handicap, physical disabilities or other special reasons. The code of guidance suggests that this last category might include battered women without children, people at risk of racial harassment and homeless young people who are at risk of sexual or financial exploitation. In *Kelly v Monklands District Council*[1] a 16-year-old girl who had left home because of violence, had nowhere else to stay, had attempted suicide and was described by the social work department as vulnerable was accepted by the court as having priority need although there was no evidence of possible sexual or financial exploitation.

(iv) Those who are pregnant or reside with a pregnant woman.

Local authority duties. Once the authority have carried out their investigation and answered these questions they must notify the applicant of their decision and the reasons for it. Regardless of the decision the authority will have a duty to provide some form of assistance to the applicant. The nature of that assistance will depend on how the questions have been answered:

1 1986 SLT 169.

(a) They have a duty to provide advice and appropriate assistance where either:
   (i) they are satisfied that the applicant is homeless threatened with homelessness but are not satisfied that he/she has priority need; or
   (ii) where the applicant does have priority need but became homeless or threatened with homelessness intentionally.

(b) Where the applicant is intentionally homeless they have a duty to secure the provision of accommodation for the applicant for such a period as will give him/her a reasonable opportunity to secure permanent accommodation. The code of guidance suggests a period of 28 days.

(c) They have a duty to take reasonable steps to ensure that accommodation does not cease to become available to the applicant where he/she has priority need and is threatened with homelessness but this is not intentional.

(d) They have a duty to secure that accommodation becomes available to an applicant who has priority need and is unintentionally homeless. This obligation is only to **secure** the provision of accommodation, the actual provision may be done by someone other than the housing authority. Any accommodation provided must not be overcrowded and must not pose a threat to the health of the occupants.

Local connection. A local connection is a connection arising from voluntary residence, from employment, from family connections or from other special circumstances. Where neither the applicant nor any member of his/her family has a local connection with the area where the application is made, but they do have such a connection with another area in Great Britain the housing authority to whom application is made can refer the case to the authority for this second area. This can only happen if the first authority comes under an obligation to secure the provision of accommodation to the applicant. It is subject to the further requirement that there must be no risk of domestic violence to the applicant or any member of the household if they move back to the second area.

If the notified authority accepts that there is a local connection and no risk of domestic violence, the obligation to secure housing devolves on them. If this is not accepted the duty remains with the notifying authority, who, in any event, have a duty to provide temporary housing while this decision is made.

Note that the legislation refers to a local connection in Great Britain, a local connection in Northern Ireland would therefore be irrelevant.

Conclusion. It is important to note in this area of law that housing authorities have wide discretionary powers and therefore that the policies of individual authorities are as important as the statutory framework. A knowledge of these policies is thus as vital as a knowledge of the statutory framework, particularly since research suggests wide variation in practice, though this may have been moderated by the new code of guidance[1].

It should also be noted that there is no statutory appeal against the decision of a local authority on a homelessness application, although most local authorities do run some form of informal appeal mechanism. Often the only recourse for a dissatisfied applicant is to seek judicial review of the decision. The obvious disadvantage of this is that the grounds for review are limited and do not permit a re-examination of the merits of the case[2].

The Morris Committee emphasised that homelessness was an area in which 'there is an overwhelming need for effective cooperation between the two services [social work and housing]'[3]. The importance of co-operation is further stressed in the code of guidance which identifies a role for social work in, for example, the initial inquiries (in *Kelly* (above) the court stressed the need for the housing authority to take into account information from the social work department in reaching their decision), in preventing arrears and evictions, and in providing support for rehoused families.

Since housing is a perpetually scarce resource and housing authorities are normally organised following the rules of large bureaucracies, it may well be justified and acceptable to both client and social worker for the social worker to take an active role in assisting the client with an application and in being supportive throughout the process. Accommodation provided, particularly temporary accommodation, can prove to be an additional source of anxiety and stress for people and so further warrant the involvement of a social worker.

Through the provision of a comprehensive initial inquiry report, the social worker may provide relevant information highlighting the factors which are significant in determining the client's eligibility. Some of these include availability of suitable accommodation, reasons for threatened/homelessness, responsibility for dependent persons, presence of persons vulnerable through various risks, emergency conditions, pregnancy, and local connection.

1 G Duguid *Homelessness in Scotland*, Scottish Office Central Research Unit Papers (1990).
2 See ch 1, pt 13.
3 *Housing and social work: a joint approach* SDD 1975 para 8.2.

The social worker may advise the client that the housing authority may charge them for accommodation provided, that it has a duty to safeguard the property of a homeless person, and that it is an offence to give inaccurate information or to withhold information from the authority.

3. BENEFITS

(1) Contributory benefits

Entitlement to contributory benefits is based on payment of contributions through the national insurance system and the requirements vary from benefit to benefit. In most cases the contributions are made by the person entitled to benefit, the exception being widow's benefits which can be obtained on the basis of the late husband's contributions. The main contributory benefits are:

(a) Unemployment benefit

This is payable during any period of unemployment exceeding three days, and is payable for 312 days. In order to qualify the applicant must be available for and actively seeking work.

(b) Statutory sick pay and sickness benefit

Statutory sick pay (SSP) is payable for the first 28 weeks of absence from work. Employees who do not qualify for SSP and who are absent from work because of illness will be entitled to sickness benefit. After 38 weeks the entitlement becomes an entitlement to invalidity benefit.

(c) Statutory maternity pay and maternity allowance

Pregnant women who have worked for the same employer for 6 months ending with the 14th week before confinement will normally be entitled to statutory maternity pay. The normal period of entitlement is 18 weeks starting on the 11th week before confinement. Women who do not qualify for SMP will be entitled to maternity allowance if they have worked for 6 out of the previous 12 months.

(d) Widows' benefits

Widowed women may be entitled to a lump sum widow's payment, a widowed mother's allowance if they are also in receipt of child benefit, or a widow's pension.

(e) Retirement pensions

Retirement pensions are payable to men over 65 and women over 60. Entitlement is generally dependant on fulfilment of contribution conditions.

(2) Non-contributory benefits

As their name suggests entitlement to these benefits does not depend on having made contributions through National Insurance. Unlike the contributory benefits, however, many of them are means-tested.

(a) Income support

Income support is available to those aged 18 or over not in full-time work and who qualify on income and capital grounds. People between 16 and 18 should in theory be provided with a training place thus obviating the need for income support. In practice, however, the availability of such places is subject to some limitation. The age limit is subject to some limited exceptions, eg a 16 or 17-year-old who cannot work because of disability or is a single parent.

For the purposes of income support and family credit a person is in full-time work if he/she is working more than 16 hours per week. People with capital in excess of £8,000 are not entitled to income support and deductions from the amount receivable are made for any savings in excess of £3,000. The payment consists of a basic allowance supplemented by premiums available in particular circumstances, eg for children, lone parents and disability.

(b) Family credit

Family credit is designed to assist families with a member in work. It is subject to the same income and capital limits as income support. In addition, to qualify, either the claimant or his/her partner must be in full-time employment and must be responsible for a child or young person.

(c) Child benefit

Child benefit is payable to the mother of any child under 16, or under 19 if undergoing full-time education up to A level or equivalent standard.

(d) Attendance allowance

Attendance allowance is designed to help to pay for assistance to a person over 65 or who is disabled at age 65 or over who needs help with his/her personal care, eg help with washing, dressing or going to the toilet.

(e) Disability living allowance

This is a benefit for people under 65 who need assistance with personal care because of a disability or illness, or who cannot walk or have difficulty in walking because of disability or illness. People in employment who cannot earn as much as they otherwise would may be entitled to claim disability working allowance if they are in receipt of disability living allowance or certain other benefits.

(f) Invalid care allowance

This can be claimed by someone over the age of 16 who is regularly and substantially (ie for more than 35 hours per week) involved in caring for someone who is in receipt of disability living allowance or attendance allowance. There is an income limit for this benefit and those in full-time education cannot claim.

(g) Severe disability allowance

This can be claimed by someone who has been unable to work for 28 weeks and cannot claim Sickness Benefit or Invalidity Benefit because he/she has not paid sufficient contributions. The limiting factor is that if the incapacity starts after the 20th birthday the claimant will not be eligible unless he/she is 80% disabled.

(h) Housing benefit

Housing benefit is available to people who qualify for income support and others who qualify on income and capital grounds and is designed to give assistance with the costs of renting accommodation. Assistance with other housing costs, eg mortgage payments, is available through a premium added to income support.

(i) Community charge benefit

This benefit is available to assist in payment of the community charge and is subject to the same income and capital limits as housing benefit. The maximum level of assistance is 80% of the community charge.

(j) Social fund

The social fund exists to provide single payments to claimants in certain circumstances. Payments fall into three categories:

(i) Payments for maternity expenses, funeral expenses and cold weather. These payments are dependent on entitlement to other benefits, are not repayable and can be claimed as of right by those fulfilling the qualifying conditions.
(ii) Community care grants are available to assist in the process of re-establishment in the community after discharge from institutional or residential care or to keep someone in the community and prevent him/her going into care. They are not repayable, but are discretionary.
(iii) Budgeting and crisis loans are entirely at the discretion of local social fund officers and are cash limited on an office basis. Budgeting loans are to meet exceptional intermittent expenses. Crisis loans are to meet expenses in an emergency. These loans are repayable by deduction from benefits.

(3) Appeals and review

Initial decisions on entitlement to non-social fund benefits are mainly taken by an adjudication officer. His/her decision can be appealed to a Social Security Appeal Tribunal (SSAT) within three months. Further appeal can be made to a social security commissioner on a point of law, and then to the Court of Session. This procedure also applies to payments for funeral and maternity expenses under the social fund.

There is no right of appeal against other social fund decisions. The initial decision is made by a social fund officer. The claimant can ask him/her to **review** that decision and can then seek a further review by a social fund inspector. The only mechanism for involving an outside body is by way of seeking judicial review of the decision.

Medical questions are decided by other bodies.

Decisions on housing and community charge benefits are taken by district and islands councils. Claimants have a right to ask the council to review its decision and then to seek a review by a local review board.

(4) Social work roles and responsibilities

The link between material deprivation and a range of other factors which bring people to social workers is indisputable and one which cannot be ignored. It therefore follows that a basic understanding of the benefits system is a crucial component in a social worker's repertoire. Social workers have no legal mandate to become involved in benefit matters other than in pursuing the general obligation to promote social welfare, but notions of good practice suggest that until material needs are addressed, other needs are less accessible.

Most social work departments will employ people who are specialists in the benefit field but increasingly these workers are being reserved for training, promotional and consultative activities. This increases the necessity for social workers in field, group care or non-local authority settings with direct client contact to have sufficient knowledge and understanding to recognise the client's potential entitlement and to advise and support the client appropriately. It is also then important for the social worker to have access to the most current publications which are mainly published each April.

The 1986 Social Security Act brought back much discretion and reduced entitlement with the targeting of benefits. Social workers have legitimately raised concerns that the boundaries between social security and social work have shifted considerably leaving social workers increasingly dealing with material problems. In relation to the social fund some have followed the advice of the British Association of Social Workers and pursued a course of determined advocacy and some have proved more gun-shy fearing the charge of collusion with the Department of Social Security. Whatever route chosen provides a catch-22 but clearly client need and social work response to that shared identification of need is fairly uncontentious.

Appeals to SSATs (Social Security Appeals Tribunals) are not covered by the legal aid scheme and so there is a need for social workers to be familiar with what decisions may be successfully appealed and be prepared to either represent their client at the tribunal or refer the client to another resource where representation will be possible. In this context it is worth noting that there is some evidence that appellants who appear at tribunals, and even more those who are represented have a much higher chance of success[1].

4. DEBT RECOVERY

(1) Court actions

Generally speaking the process of debt recovery must be initiated by court action. In the vast majority of cases the action will be raised in the sheriff court and will take the form of a small claims action or a summary cause action. The former is available where the sum involved is less than £750, the latter for sums between £750 and £1500.

Apart from the financial limits there are a number of other differences between small claims and summary causes, principally:

(a) Legal aid is available in summary causes, but not in small claims, although assistance can be obtained through the legal advice and assistance scheme for these.
(b) Procedure in court is much more informal in small claims cases.
(c) The summons in a small claim can be served by the sheriff clerk, a summary cause summons must be served by a solicitor or sheriff officer.
(d) An individual can be represented by someone other than a solicitor at all stages in a small claim. Such representation is only possible at the first, largely formal, hearing of a summary cause.
(e) There is a restriction on the amount of expenses that can be awarded against the unsuccessful party in small claims. Currently the position is that no expenses can be awarded where the claim is for less than £200, above that there is a ceiling on the expenses that can be awarded against the unsuccessful party of £75.

Once a creditor has initiated action there are four courses of action open to the debtor:

(a) He/she can defend the action. This would be appropriate if there was a dispute about the amount owed or the quality of goods or services supplied. In order to defend the action the relevant form attached to the summons should be returned to court by the date specified there. Failure to return this form, indicating an intention to defend, will allow the creditor to obtain a judgment in his/her

1 Bell, Collison, Turner & Webber 'National Insurance Local Tribunals' (1975) *Journal of Social Policy* 1.

favour simply by means of a written minute without the need to turn up in court on the appointed day.

(b) Apply for a 'time to pay direction' permitting payment by instalments or as a lump sum at some future date. Again the relevant form must be returned to court with details of the proposal for repayment.

(c) Do nothing. The result of this is that the creditor will get a judgment in his/her favour which will require payment of the whole amount, plus any legal expenses, immediately. In this situation, and providing that a warrant has not been granted for a warrant sale (see below), the debtor can apply to the court for a time to pay order, which has the same effect as a time to pay direction.

(d) Pay the debt. If the debtor has already received a summons he/she will be liable for the creditors legal expenses.

Once a decree for the payment of money has been granted in favour of a creditor there are a number of courses of action (collectively known as diligence) open to him/her if payment is still not forthcoming. The main forms of diligence are poinding and sale, arrestment, and arrestment of earnings.

(2) Poinding and sale

Poinding involves the listing and valuation of all moveable property (basically all property except land and buildings) owned by the debtor, or owned jointly by the debtor and another person. This is followed by the sale of this property. There is now an extensive list of items exempt from poinding. These include bedding, toys, heating and cooking appliances and floor coverings, all provided that they are reasonably required for use in the dwellinghouse by someone living in the house.

Once a poinding has been carried out the articles poinded must not be removed or damaged. At this stage the debtor has the right to apply to court for recall of the poinding on the ground that it would be unduly harsh to proceed to a sale, that the total value fixed on the goods is less than their market value, or that the proceeds of the sale would not cover the expense of holding it. In this context it is worth noting that research undertaken for the Scottish Law Commission established that in about 20% of warrant sales the proceeds did not cover the expenses[1].

1 Scottish Office Central Research Unit *The Characteristics of Warrant Sales* (1980) 21.

If no payment is made and the poinding is not recalled the creditor can then apply to court for a warrant to hold a sale. The sale no longer takes place in the debtor's residence unless the debtor consents, but he/she is liable for the costs of removing the goods to the place of sale.

Any surplus raised by the sale is returned to the debtor. If part of the debt remains outstanding it is still owed to the creditor.

(3) Arrestment

Arrestment involves the freezing of assets belonging to or owed to the debtor, but which for the time being are in the hands of a third party. A common example would be money in a bank account. The effect of an arrestment is to prevent the third party dealing in any way with the property. In order for the debtor to have it released he/she must raise a separate action known as an action of furthcoming; the effect of this is to order the third party to hand over to the creditor assets to the value owed by the debtor.

(4) Arrestment of earnings

Arrestment of earnings involves an order to the debtor's employer to pay a part of the debtor's pay to the creditor. The order lasts until the debt is paid. There are statutory restrictions on the amount which can be deducted. There are two forms of arrestment of earnings: the earnings arrestment which covers ordinary debts and arrears of maintenance (ie payments of periodical allowance or aliment), and current maintenance arrestment to enforce current maintenance payments.

(5) Social work contribution

Increasingly people are finding themselves in debt. Sometimes the usual coping mechanisms fail. Some people panic and find themselves in a state of crisis. Many go to Citizen's Advice Bureaux and some go to the social work department. The Social Work (Scotland) Act 1968, section 12 umbrella with the duty to promote social welfare and ensure that the local authority is saved greater expense at a later date, requires and enables social workers to become involved with people in debt. Social workers are ideally placed to advise clients about the process of debt recovery; reminding them for example that they may be eligible for legal aid, that they must return the summons to the court if they intend to defend the debt action, that they may apply for time to make payment toward the debt, that they may be subject to diligence (poinding and sale of their property or arrestment of assets or earnings), that only certain items of property are liable to be poinded, that they need not agree to have a warrant sale in their home, that any surplus money raised in such a sale belongs to them, and that only a limited amount of money may be arrested from their earnings.

Social workers may well provide support for families suffering from the stress of these procedures. If the debtor is eligible (see the discussion of the use of section 12 funds, chapter 1, part 15), it may be possible for the social work department to provide material assistance as well. Families who have defaulted on the payment of mortgages may need advice and guidance about alternative accommodation. Increasingly people may be in a position of multiple indebtedness and it may be appropriate for a social worker to be advocating on their behalf with creditors and negotiating to combine various debts and arrange feasible payments. Debtors may also be entitled to benefit, about which a social worker might advise them.

5. DISCRIMINATION

(1) History and definitions

The earliest piece of legislation in this field was the Race Relations Act of 1965 which dealt with racial discrimination in places of public resort. A further Act was passed in 1968 and extended coverage to housing, employment, education and provision of services. The emphasis of both of these Acts was on providing a process of conciliation between the parties involved.

The earliest legislation on sex discrimination was the Equal Pay Act 1970 which requires equality of treatment in all matters relating to contracts of employment (it therefore covers such matters as holiday entitlement as well as earnings). This was not brought into force until 1975, at the same time as the Sex Discrimination Act 1975 which dealt with discrimination in other aspects of employment (for example, selection for employment, promotion and dismissal), in education, in provision of accommodation and in the provision of goods facilities and services. A further change was made in 1983 when a requirement that men and women should be paid equally for work of equal value was added to the existing requirement for equal pay for like work or work rated equally in an employer's evaluation study.

The sex discrimination legislation bans discrimination on the grounds of sex, and in terms of employment also prohibits less favourable treatment of married people.

Following doubts about the effectiveness of the earlier legislation the Race Relations Act 1976 was passed, based on the Sex Discrimination Act. It therefore covers the same areas as that Act but in addition created a criminal offence of incitement to racial hatred[1] and imposes on local authorities a duty to carry out their functions with due regard to the need to eliminate unlawful discrimination and promote equality of opportunity and good relations between different racial groups. The 1976 Act deals with discrimination against someone on the grounds of their membership of a racial group. A racial group is defined by reference to colour, race, nationality, or ethnic or national origins.

(2) Direct and indirect discrimination

The legislation prohibits both direct and indirect discrimination[2]. Direct discrimination takes place where someone is simply discriminated against on the basis of their race or sex. Indirect discrimination occurs where a general requirement is made that applies equally to everyone. If this requirement is such that members of a certain sex or racial group have less chance of meeting the requirement than others then the requirement will be indirectly discriminatory. An example of this was a case where employers had agreed with a trade union that part-time workers would be made redundant first. When the case went to an industrial tribunal this was found to amount to indirect discrimination. The reason for this was that the proportion of women who could meet the requirement for avoiding redundancy, full-time employment, was considerably less than the proportion of men who could comply.

It should also be noted that separate provision for different racial groups also amounts to discrimination.

(a) Exempted areas

There are a number of areas which are exempted from the scope of the legislation and in which discrimination is still allowed. Examples include: special treatment of women in connection with pregnancy or childbirth, entertainment (where particular characteristics are required to play a role), and provision of personal social/welfare services where this can best be done by a member of a particular sex or

1 Now contained in the Public Order Act 1986.
2 For a fuller discussion of this see L Lustgarten *Legal Control of Racial Discrimination* (1980) chs 1 and 2.

racial group. In addition special provision can be made to meet the special needs of a racial group in relation to education, training or welfare. This would, for example, allow for the provision of special training to allow people to obtain the qualifications required for a particular job, but it does not allow for positive discrimination in selection for employment.

(b) *Remedies*

Complaints regarding discrimination in employment are dealt with by industrial tribunals. All other cases are dealt with in Scotland by the sheriff court. In addition the Acts set up an Equal Opportunities Commission for sex equality cases and a Commission for Racial Equality for race relations. The functions of both of these bodies are similar and are to give advice and assistance to those bringing cases, and to carry out formal investigations into particular bodies or areas of activity. They also have the sole right to enforce the provisions relating to discrimination in advertising, pressure to discriminate and instructions or inducements to discriminate.

(3) Control of immigration

This brief section looks at an area of law which is closely related to the Race Relations Act. As one commentator has noted 'Perhaps the most subversive influence on the success of the [Race Relations Act] is the existence of the quite contradictory assumptions of the immigration laws and the kind of racialist propaganda which is associated with them'[1].

Apart from British citizens[2] and European communities nationals all other entrants into Britain are subject to immigration control. In some cases, for example visitors, this simply requires production of a passport, in other cases, eg those wishing to settle in the United Kingdom, entry clearance must be obtained in the country of origin before coming to the United Kingdom.

Those refused entry have a right of appeal to an adjudicator and then to the Immigration Appeal Tribunal. These rights of appeal can, however, only be exercised once the appellant has left the United Kingdom. In addition the entrant has the right to seek judicial review of a refusal of entry, but this no longer guarantees that the applicant

1 I Macdonald *Race Relations: the New Law* (1977), p 8.
2 No attempt is made here to enter the complex area of law relating to nationality.

will be allowed to stay in the United Kingdom pending the hearing. Finally Members of Parliament have the right to ask the immigration service to reconsider a decision to send someone back, however they no longer have the power to prevent removal from the United Kingdom.

Entrants other than those admitted for settlement will be subject to conditions, eg, visitors may only stay for six months. Deportation can be ordered for breach of such conditions and it can also be ordered by the Secretary of State if he deems it to be conducive to the public good and it can be recommended by a court following a conviction. There is a right of appeal against a deportation order.

(4) Social work contribution

The legislative similarity in the treatment of racial and sexual discrimination has been capitalised upon for reasons of simplicity and clarity. For the practitioner, however, matters are never that straightforward. Some would argue that social workers are immersed in patriarchal structures which foster institutional sexism and racism[1] and while there may well be a daily accumulation of evidence for these assertions, what is of interest here is an acknowledgement of the likely effects of such structures upon social work practice.

Although there are no statutory obligations for social workers in the area of discrimination, except for the duty to carry out their functions with due regard to the need to eliminate unlawful discrimination and promote equality of opportunity and good relations between different racial groups, they are sometimes involved with people who are experiencing deprivation at least in part due to discrimination.

In Scotland, this discrimination may also take the form of sectarianism or even classism as when individuals from peripheral housing estates are excluded from employment purely on the basis of assumptions made about them on the basis of their surname or address. These forms of discrimination are not the subject of specific legislation but can possibly be addressed through more general legislative provisions. One central tenet of social work values is the adherence to the view that men and women are individuals who must be accorded respect regardless of their particular traits or actions[2]. The implementation of this stance requires social workers to maintain a sensitivity and vigilance to matters of discrimination of all description and to use

1 See for example J Dale and P Foster in *Feminists and State Welfare* (1986), and L Dominelli in *Anti-racist Social Work* (1988).
2 See for example R Plant *Social and Moral Theory in Casework* (1970), p 12.

the regulatory and enabling functions of the law in this area to facilitate the improvement of their clients' quality of life.

Some areas which social work touches upon have provided particular evidence of discriminatory practice and might require special attention. These include sentencing policy in the criminal justice system[1], immigration decisions, allocation of council houses, and fostering and adoption policy. The professional qualification for social work, the Diploma in Social Work, requires that social work 'students are prepared not only for ethnically sensitive practice but also to challenge and confront institutional and other forms of racism...[and] to combat other forms of discrimination based on age, gender, sexual orientation, class, disability, culture or creed'.[2] It is also incumbent upon educational establishments and social work agencies providing practice placements for students to demonstrate an adherence to these principles.

6. ACCESS TO INFORMATION

(1) Introduction

There are now a number of pieces of legislation which allow for access by individuals to records which contain information regarding them. Two of these, the Data Protection Act 1984 and the Access to Personal Files Act 1987 have direct relevance to social work practice and should perhaps be considered as what we have termed 'professional law' in part 1 above. These will be considered in some detail below. The rest of the legislation gives rights of access to a variety of information and will be considered more briefly.

(2) Data Protection Act 1984

This legislation only covers information held in such a form that it can be processed by equipment operating automatically. It therefore does not cover information which is recorded in written files and records. In general terms people who hold the former type of information must register with the Data Protection Registrar and must give individuals access to information kept about them. There are restrictions on

1 See for example P Carlen and A Worrall (eds) *Gender, Crime and Justice* (1987).
2 Central Council for Education and Training in Social Work Paper 30 – *Requirements and Regulations for the Diploma in Social Work* (1989).

access to certain types of information, one of these being information kept for the purposes, or acquired in the course, of carrying out social work.

Briefly these restrictions prevent the disclosure of information where it would be likely to cause serious harm to the physical, mental or emotional condition of the person applying for access, or anyone else, or where the identity of someone else, other than a social worker or person who has consented to disclosure, would be disclosed as a result of disclosure of the information. In addition where the information includes information as to the health of the applicant which has been supplied by a doctor or other 'health professional' (see below) that health professional must be consulted before the information is disclosed.

This legislation will be of increasing relevance to social workers as local authority departments establish client data bases and use computer files as an alternative to paper files.

(3) Access to Personal Files Act 1987

The Access to Personal Files Act 1987 permits access to what it describes as 'personal information' held either by housing authorities (including Scottish Homes) for the purpose of tenancies or by regions and islands for the purpose of their functions under the Social Work (Scotland) Act 1968. Unlike the Data Protection Act the Access to Personal Files Act does not extend to voluntary organisations; there is, therefore, no statutory right of access to the information covered by the latter Act which is kept by voluntary organisations, although most will operate policies which permit access.

'Personal information' is defined as information relating to a living individual who can be identified from that information or from that and other information in the possession of the authority. The right of access extends to any expression of an opinion about the individual concerned, but not any expression of intention (for example, plans for future care of or action in respect of the person). Access is not restricted to information kept in a form which can be processed automatically as with the Data Protection Act 1984, but extends to information held in any form. The main restriction is that the right of access does not extend to any information recorded before the date when the regulations filling in the detail of access arrangements came into effect. In the case of social work that date is 1 April 1989. Earlier information may, however, **have** to be disclosed if this is necessary to make sense of information recorded after that date. Local authorities also have the power to disclose such earlier information.

The person entitled to access is the person to whom the information relates. Minor children, ie boys aged 14 or over and girls aged 12 or over, have a right of access to information about them and would have to consent to any application by their parents for information about them.

The detail of the access arrangements for social work is contained in the Access to Personal Files (Social Work)(Scotland) Regulations 1989[1]. In addition most authorities will have their own procedures and guidelines for dealing with access to information which will, for example, set out their policy on disclosure and the procedure for dealing with requests for information.

Under the regulations the social work authority is obliged to tell anyone who applies in the correct form whether they hold any personal information about him/her and, subject to the restrictions on access described below, the contents of that information. The information must be provided in an intelligible form. The time limit for supplying this information is generally 40 days from the date of receipt of the application, though this period can be extended, for example if the authority needs further information from the applicant to process the application.

As mentioned, there are certain restrictions on, or exemptions from, disclosure. These release authorities from disclosing only that information which falls within the exemptions; any other personal information held by the authority must be disclosed. This may involve, for example, the deletion of information identifying a third party from a file before the applicant is allowed to see it (unless, of course, the third party consents to disclosure). The exemptions fall into three categories:

(a) Information as to the physical or mental health of the applicant. Where information of this nature is held by a social work authority and has, or is believed to have, originated from or been supplied by a health professional the authority must advise the relevant health board (if the health professional is employed by a health board) or the health professional of the request for information. The term health professional is defined widely and includes not only doctors, dentists, opticians and nurses, but also registered chiropodists and physiotherapists, clinical psychologists, speech therapists, health visitors, and art or music therapists employed by a health board.

The social work authority is exempted from disclosing the information

1 SI 1989/251.

if, within the 40 day period mentioned above, the health board or health professional informs them that disclosure would either:

(i) cause serious harm to the physical or mental health of the applicant or any other person; or

(ii) reveal to the applicant the identity of some other person other than a health professional or someone who has consented to disclosure.

It should be noted that if there is no response within the 40 day period the social work authority must disclose the information, even if it would have one of the effects specified.

(b) Information from reporters to children's panels. Before information supplied by or originating from a reporter can be disclosed the reporter must be informed of the request for information. The social work authority will be exempted from the obligation to disclose the information if, within the 40 day period, the reporter advises them that it should not be disclosed because this would be likely either:

(i) to cause serious harm to the physical or mental health of the applicant or any other person; or

(ii) to disclose to the applicant the identity of another person who has not consented to disclosure; or

(iii) to prejudice the prevention or detection of a crime or the apprehension or prosecution of offenders.

Once again if there is no response within the forty day period the information must be disclosed.

In this context it is worth noting that there is a right of access under the regulations to any social background report prepared for a children's hearing. This is subject, of course, to the restriction on information from the Reporter considered here and to obtaining any necessary consents from third parties (see below)[1].

(c) Other information. The social work authority is also exempted from disclosing information which falls into one of the following categories:

(i) information which, if disclosed, would be likely to prejudice the carrying on of the authority's social work functions because it is likely to cause serious harm to the physical or mental health or the emotional condition of the applicant or any other person; or

(ii) information which would reveal the identity of another individual who is not an employee of the social work department or a provider of services for reward to the department (eg an approved foster parent in receipt of a fostering allowance) and who has not consented to disclosure; or

1 See also ch 4, pt 4(2).

(iii) information which, if disclosed, would be likely to prejudice the prevention or detection of crime or the apprehension or prosecution of offenders; or
(iv) information in respect of which a claim of confidentiality between client and professional legal adviser could be maintained in legal proceedings; or
(v) information covered by certain statutory provisions, mainly information to do with adoption and a child's record of needs.

There are three points worth noting briefly about this third category of exemptions. The first is that one of the concerns is the protection of confidentiality. Information which would identify a third party as the source, or which relates in part to that third party must not be disclosed without his/her consent. The second is that there is no time limit for the consent as there is in the case of responses on health information and information from the reporter. The information cannot therefore be revealed simply because the 40 day period has passed without response. Thirdly, where there is no response from a health board/health professional/reporter the authority cannot fall back on one of the exemptions in this category to refuse disclosure. This final category does not extend to information covered by the previous two categories.

Rights to correction

Anyone who has obtained access to information held about him/her can serve a notice on the authority requiring them to correct or delete any information which he/she regards as inaccurate. If they are not satisfied that the information is incorrect the authority are not bound to amend their records, but the individual concerned has the right to have a note that he/she regards the information as inaccurate placed with the information (in practice this would, for example, be noted on the file).

Anyone who is the subject of information held by a social work authority and who is unhappy with any decision taken by the authority about access to information or rectification of information has the right to seek review of the decision. The review is carried out by a committee of three councillors.

(4) Other legislation

(a) Access to Medical Reports Act 1988

This gives a right of access to medical reports prepared for employment or insurance purposes.

(b) Consumer Credit Act 1974

This Act gives a consumer the right to obtain a copy of any file relating to him/her kept by a credit reference agency. The right is to see any information, however it is held. If the consumer considers that any of the information is incorrect and may lead to prejudice he/she may serve a notice on the agency requiring them to correct or delete the information. If the agency refuses to do this the consumer can apply to the Director General of Fair Trading to exercise his/her enforcement powers. The information kept by credit reference agencies often turns out to be incorrect and this may be a remedy worth pursuing where someone is refused credit or some other service because of an adverse report from an agency.

(c) Access to Health Records Act 1989

This gives a right of access to health records kept by health professionals (see above). Application is made to the holder of the record, eg a general practitioner or the health board. There is no right of access where the patient is incapable of understanding the nature of the application, where the patient is a child and the granting of access is not in the best interests of the child (unless he/she has consented to the application), and where the information was recorded before 1 November 1991, unless this information is necessary to understand information recorded later. There are also exemptions covering information likely to cause serious damage to the mental or physical health of the patient or another individual, and information identifying a third party who is not a health professional and who has not consented to disclosure. There is provision for application to be made for correction of health records and for a statement of the patients position to be included in the record if correction is not made.

(d) Access to school records

The School Pupil Records (Scotland) Regulations 1990[1] give a right of access to personal information kept by education authorities in the context of providing school education. There are certain exemptions to the right of access, these include exemptions similar to categories *(a)*, *(b)* and *(c)* *(iii)* and *(iv)* noted above in relation to social work information, as well as references for employment and information which would disclose the identities of third parties. The rights to seek correction and review are similar to those noted above for social work information.

1 SI 1990/1551.

7. EDUCATION

This section is intended to deal briefly with the rights and duties of parents and discipline in schools. The principal right that parents have in relation to education is the right, subject to availability of places, to choose the school where their child will be educated. The principal duty of parents is to ensure that their child receives a suitable education while of school age; this may be done at home, or by sending him/her to an independent school or, most commonly, to a local authority school. Failure to meet this responsibility can result in an attendance order being served requiring the child to attend a specific school or in prosecution of the parents. The child may be referred to the reporter for the children's hearing as being in need of compulsory measures of care if he/she fails to attend school regularly without a reasonable excuse[1].

A child may no longer be subjected to corporal punishment in school, but may be disciplined in other ways, eg additional homework or verbal reprimand. In serious cases the child may be excluded from school, if this happens the parents must be notified right away and there is a right of appeal against the exclusion.

Children with special educational needs are dealt with in chapter 5, part 3.

1 See ch 4, pt 4.

3. Children and their families

1. THE RIGHTS AND POWERS OF PARENTS AND CHILDREN

(1) Introduction

This section starts with an attempt to explain the powers and rights that a child has at different stages of his/her life. Powers are concerned with the ability or capacity of children to enter into legal transactions, for example contracts, and to give legally effective agreement, eg the giving of consent to medical treatment. Rights are concerned with the child's rights to make choices about his/her life, eg choices about friends, about religious beliefs and about where to stay. The extent of a child's rights is closely connected with the extent of the parental rights held by his or her parent(s): the child's power to control his/her own life grows with the decline of the parents' rights. For this reason we will also consider the rights of parents in this section.

The age of majority, the age at which, technically, one is fully an adult, is 18 in Scotland. There are other age limits relevant for other purposes. For example, at the age of 16 one can marry and enter into other legal transactions (see below). 16 is also the age at which compulsory education finishes and below which children can be referred to a children's hearing and be the subject of actions for custody or access (see below). Children under the age of eight cannot be guilty of a criminal offence or be referred to a children's hearing on the ground that they have committed an offence.

Below the age of 18 the historically important division was between pupils and minors. Pupils are boys under 14 and girls under 12, minors are those between those ages and 18. Pupils had very restricted powers and were subject to the control and guidance of their tutor, normally their parent. Minors had slightly greater powers, for example to enter contracts and to consent to some types of medical treatment, and acted with the concurrence of a curator, again usually the parent. Where a child had two parents (in the legal sense, see below) both were tutor/curator of the child.

The Age of Legal Capacity (Scotland) Act 1991 made some changes to this position. In particular it made changes which affect the capacity of children and abolished tutors and curators, creating instead the position of guardian who, in relation to children under the age of 16, was to have the powers of a tutor. These developments are discussed in more detail below, but it should be noted that although the distinction between pupils and minors is generally no longer relevant as far as the powers or capacity of children is concerned it is still relevant, as we shall see, as far as children's rights are concerned.

Knowledge and an understanding of the law in this area should prove invaluable to social workers and young persons, for example, leaving care and planning for independent living, entering into contractual arrangements eg with catalogue companies, on home supervision and perhaps in conflict with parents, or in care and needing to know what rights and responsibilities are relevant.

(2) Legal capacity of children

The Age of Legal Capacity (Scotland) Act 1991 now contains the law relating to the capacity of children. In terms of this Act the important age is 16. Below this age, subject to the exceptions noted below, children have no capacity to enter into what the Act calls 'transactions'. The term 'transactions' includes contractual agreements, the giving of any consent having legal effect (for example consent to medical treatment), and the bringing or defending of any legal action in a civil court.

The main exceptions are:

(a) Children under 16 may enter into transactions of a kind normally entered into by children of the child in question's age and circumstances, provided the terms of the transaction are reasonable.
(b) Children over the age of 12 have the power to make wills.
(c) A child under 16 may consent to any surgical, medical or dental procedure or treatment[1] where, in the opinion of the medical practitioner attending him or her, the child is capable of understanding the nature and possible consequences of the procedure or treatment. This is considered more fully below.
(d) Children over 12 have the power to consent (or withhold consent) to adoption and freeing for adoption.
(e) The exclusion regarding civil court action is specifically stated to be without prejudice to the law existing before the Act came into

1 This would include consenting to the prescribing of contraceptives.

operation which allowed pupils and minors to institute legal proceedings either directly or acting through a *curator ad litem*[1].

Children over the age of 16 have full legal capacity in respect of the matters covered by the Act. 16 and 17-year-olds enjoy some additional protection in that they can challenge any transactions entered into at those ages before their 21st birthday on the grounds that the transaction was prejudicial.

As we have noted a child can now give effective consent to medical treatment if he/she is capable of understanding the nature and possible consequences of the treatment, with the judgement as to ability to understand being made by the doctor or dentist treating the child. This statement of the law still leaves two areas of difficulty. The first of these is: what happens when there is conflict between the wishes of the parent and the wishes of the child? What rights does a parent have in such a situation? Logic would suggest that since children are now specifically given the capacity to consent to treatment on their own behalf, the rights of parents would cease when the child is old enough to exercise this capacity in relation to a particular type of treatment. The question is not free from doubt however. In the recent English case *Re R (a minor)* the suggestion was made that if a child consented to medical treatment the parent could not overrule that consent, but if the child refused treatment the parent could override the refusal and consent on the child's behalf[2]. This suggestion has now been extended to 16 and 17-year-olds.[3]

The second area of difficulty is what happens where the child is unable to consent and the parents refuse to consent to therapeutic treatment? In such cases there is guidance from the Scottish Home and Health Department authorising doctors to treat the child in certain circumstances. There is also the possibility, noted below, of applying to court for permission for treatment under section 3 of the Law Reform (Parent and Child)(Scotland) Act 1986. Failure on the part of the parent to consent to therapeutic treatment may also give rise to a referral to a children's hearing on the ground of lack of parental care[4].

In emergency cases treatment can be given without consent.

(3) Parental rights

Following from the definition provided by the Law Reform (Parent and Child)(Scotland) Act 1986 parental rights have been described as

1 See *Ward v Walker* 1920 1 SLT 2.
2 [1991] 4 All ER 177 at 186 e-f.
3 *Re J (a minor)* (Medical Treatment), *The Guardian*, 22 July 1992.
4 *Finlayson, Applicant* 1989 SCLR 601. See ch 4, pt 3(4).

the rights of guardianship, custody, access, and a bundle of residual rights, some derived from the common law and others derived from Acts of Parliament. These rights, which we will consider more fully below, are conferred on those whom the law regards as the parents of a child. As far as the law is concerned the parents of a child are the child's mother and the child's father, provided that he was married to the mother at the date of conception of the child or subsequently. A father who is not married to the mother can take advantage of the provisions considered below and apply to court to be granted parental rights. Where more than one person has parental rights in respect of a child each person can exercise these rights independently of the other. For example, if the parents are separated, the mother can take any decision about the child without consulting the father.

As we have seen, guardianship replaced the rights of tutory and curatory. It has been defined as the parent's

> 'right to manage the child's property, enter into contracts on the child's behalf, litigate on the child's behalf, and generally to act on the child's behalf in any legally relevant matter where the child is incapable of acting on his or her own behalf. The parent as guardian is the child's administrator-in-law or legal representative. Guardianship lasts until the child is 16.'[1]

Custody is the right to have a child under the age of 16 living with the parent and to control the child's day to day upbringing.

Access is the right to reasonable contact with a child enjoyed by a parent who does not have custody or care of the child.

The residual category includes the right to attend a children's hearing involving the child, the right to appoint a guardian to take over parental rights in the event of the parent's death, control of the child's religion and education, consent to medical treatment, discipline, choice of name and choice of residence. With the exception of the first two, these rights are rights which derive from having custody of the child.

As this list indicates, parental rights over children are extensive, although they are linked to and limited by parental duties and responsibilities. Specific parental duties will be mentioned below, but there is a more general limit on parents' exercise of their rights; that is that the purpose of conferring rights on parents is to allow them to fulfil their responsibilities towards their children. This was expressed by Lord Scarman in the case of *Gillick v West Norfolk and Wisbech Area Health Authority*[2] where he said: 'The principle is that parental

1 Scottish Law Commission *Report on Family Law* HC (1992/93) no 4 para 2.15.
2 [1985] 3 All ER 402, 421d.

right or power of control of the person and property of the child exists primarily to enable the parent to discharge his duty of maintenance, protection and education until [the child] reaches such an age as to be able to look after himself and make his own decisions.' In England and Wales the Children Act 1989 recasts parental rights as parental responsibilities for this reason, and the Scottish Law Commission has proposed that new legislation should make it clear that parental rights are conferred to enable parents to fulfil their parental responsibilities.

The extension of tutory to children under the age of 16 in the form of guardianship gave rise to concerns that this amounted to an extension of parental rights over children above the age of minority. The concern arose from the fact that children over that age had rights, eg as to choice of religion, association and access to files, not enjoyed by pupil children. The fear was that parents as guardians would gain rights to control these aspects of children's lives up to the age of 16 which they did not previously have. The consensus now appears to be that the fears are unfounded and that parents' rights to control these aspects of a child's upbringing derive from custody, not from tutory, so the extension of tutory did not change parents' rights in these areas. It is only fair to say, however, that this consensus is not universal. Professor Walker, for example, has expressed the view that 'Tutory is the power and faculty to **govern the person**, and to manage the estate of a pupil...'[1].

An understanding of parental rights and duties, and of the rights of children, is of particular importance for understanding the position of a local authority which assumes parental rights[2] and the position of children in care where parental rights have not been assumed[3].

(4) Children's rights

As we have already noted, as children get older the rights of their parents diminish, and the rights of the child to manage his/her affairs and take decisions about his/her life increase. This is particularly the case with children over the age of minority, which therefore still has relevance in terms of the acquisition of rights rather than legal capacity.

A specific right that children possess is the right to support from their parents, or, indeed, from anyone who has accepted them as a member of their family. This right to support or aliment lasts until the

1 *Principles of Scottish Private Law* (4th edn, 1982) vol I, 305, emphasis added.
2 See ch 4, pt 2.
3 See ch 4, pt 6(5).

child is 18, or until the age of 25 if the 'child' is undertaking full time education.

(5) Parental duties

The general parental duty in relation to the upbringing of children has already been noticed. But parents also have more specific duties, for example to ensure that their children are provided with education if of school age, and to provide financial support. This duty to provide financial support extends to children under 16 in the care of the local authority[1].

(6) Parental rights in the courts

Any of the parental rights listed above can be the subject of a court action. In any such action involving parental rights the paramount consideration is the best interests of the child or children involved.

The most common cases about parental rights concern custody and access. In many instances the case will be one of divorce or separation and the parties will have agreed arrangements as to custody or access which the court will endorse.

Actions for custody alone may, in common with any other action relating to parental rights, be brought by anyone having an interest. Where the action for custody is brought by anyone other than a parent of the child the local authority must be notified of the action and must produce a report for the court on all the circumstances of the child and on the proposed arrangements for his/her upbringing[2]. The Children Act 1975 contains a detailed set of requirements as to the time the child must have resided with the applicant before an application for custody can be granted; the detail is, however, unnecessary as the court can grant an application for custody if the applicant can show cause why the application should be granted[3].

In custody actions the court has the power, in exceptional cases, to place the child in the care of the local authority[4] or to place the child under the supervision of the local authority[5].

Section 3 of the Law Reform (Parent and Child)(Scotland) Act 1986

1 1968 Act, s78.
2 See also pt 2(6).
3 Children Act 1975, s47(2)(d).
4 Matrimonial Proceedings (Children) Act 1958, s10; Guardianship Act 1973, s11.
5 Matrimonial Proceedings (Children) Act 1958, s12; Guardianship Act 1973, s11. See also ch 4, pt 5(2).

gives a wide range of people the right to apply to court for a broad range of parental rights. It provides that 'any person claiming an interest may make application to the court for an order relating to parental rights and the court may make such an order relating to parental rights as it thinks fit.'

This seems to confer on a wide range of people (those claiming an interest) the right to seek any sort of order regarding any area of parental rights. It has been suggested, for example, that it would entitle a doctor or social worker to apply for the right to consent to medical treatment for a child where the child's parents were refusing to agree to therapeutic treatment. It may also allow parents whose parental rights have been assumed by a local authority to challenge actions and decisions in respect of their child by the local authority[1].

2. MARRIAGE, SEPARATION AND DIVORCE

(1) Marriage

Before two people can get married certain requirements must be fulfilled. Both parties must be over 16, must be single, must not be within the forbidden degrees of relationship and one must be male and the other female. If these requirements are met the parties will generally go through a regular marriage, ie a religious ceremony or civil wedding. It is, however, possible to become husband and wife without such a ceremony. Such a marriage is referred to as an irregular marriage and the only way in which it can now take place is the process of cohabitation with habit and repute. For this the parties must live together and be regarded as husband and wife for a sufficient period of time. On its own, cohabitation does not constitute the marriage. This must be formalised by applying to the Court of Session for a declarator of marriage[2].

Irregular marriage is a true form of common law marriage, ie it has no statutory basis, and should be clearly distinguished from what are commonly referred to as 'common law' marriages. These situations, where, for example, a man is referred to as being a woman's common law husband, amount to mere cohabitation and do not give rise to the legal consequences which follow from a proper marriage. For

1 Notwithstanding the decision in *Beagley v Beagley* 1984 SLT 202, which was concerned only with custody and access and was decided before the passing of the Act: though see *F v F* 1991 SLT 357.

2 For a recent example see *Donnelly v Donnelly's Executor* 1992 SLT 13, which involved cohabitation over a period of about eight years.

example, the father of a child who is actually married to the mother will have parental rights in respect of that child, whereas the 'common law' husband who fathers a child will not automatically have parental rights and will have to apply to court for them.

After marriage the parties have a mutual obligation of financial support and an obligation to live together as man and wife.

(2) Separation

It is possible to obtain a formal judicial separation requiring the parties to a marriage to live apart, but in general any separation will be informal, as will any arrangements for aliment or custody of or access to any children. If such informal arrangements are impossible it may be necessary to take action in the sheriff court to regulate these matters.

(3) Divorce

The Divorce (Scotland) Act 1976 introduced a single ground for divorce in Scotland: 'irretrievable breakdown of the marriage'. In effect this simply amounted to a restatement of the existing grounds of divorce, since they, together with two new grounds based on non-cohabitation, were to be evidence of breakdown.

The five grounds evidencing an irretrievable breakdown are:

(a) Adultery.
(b) Behaviour – where the defender 'has behaved . . . in such a way that the pursuer cannot reasonably be expected to cohabit with the defender.' This ground would cover violence by the defender, drunkenness or unnatural, excessive or insufficient sexual demands.
(c) Desertion – where the defender has left without good cause and has been absent for a period of two years.
(d) Two years non-cohabitation with consent – where the parties have not lived together as husband and wife for two years and the defender consents to the divorce.
(e) Five years non-cohabitation – here the defender's consent is not required.

(4) Divorce procedure

Prior to 1984 divorce could only be obtained in the Court of Session. Since May of that year it has also been possible to divorce in the sheriff court, and that is where most cases are now dealt with.

There are two types of procedure by which a divorce can be obtained: ordinary and simplified. The ordinary procedure is similar to that involved in an ordinary court action.

The simplified procedure amounts essentially to a do-it-yourself divorce. It is only available where the divorce is based on non-cohabitation, there are no children of the marriage under 16, and no financial provisions are being sought. An application is completed and returned to the clerk of the court (either the sheriff court or Court of Session) who notifies the other party. If there is no dispute a decree of divorce will arrive through the post after a short while.

(5) Financial provision on divorce

Financial provision on divorce is often regulated by agreement between the parties, failing which the Family Law (Scotland) Act 1985 sets out a number of rules and principles to guide courts in making financial provision. The general effect of these guidelines is to discourage orders for periodical allowance over a long period of time which would maintain a link between the parties. Instead the Act favours a clean break. To this end it envisages that the principal form of settlement on divorce will be transfer of property or the payment of a capital sum (though this payment may be staged over time).

Before the court can make any award of financial provision it must first be satisfied that the award is justified by reference to the principles contained in the Act and is reasonable having regard to the resources of the parties.

The basic principle is that the net value of the matrimonial property should be shared fairly between the parties – generally fair sharing will be equal sharing.

(6) Custody of and access to children

There are children involved in about half of all divorce actions and one of the decisions to be made by the court is on custody and access. Indeed, there is a statutory prohibition on granting divorce unless the court is satisfied that the arrangements made for the care and upbringing of any children are satisfactory or the best available in the circumstances.

In virtually all cases custody and access arrangements will have been agreed by the parties and the court will simply endorse these, although it does have an overriding duty to consider the welfare of the children before making any decision (see also part 1 above).

Culpability in the breakdown of the marriage is not relevant in the decision-making process about custody and access. Custody awards normally follow these principles: the custody of young children to the mother; the parent who had retained the custody of the child at the time of separation maintains custody; siblings are not separated; access is rarely denied to the non-custodial parent; and in awarding custody preference will be given to the parent who can provide a religious upbringing.

Social workers will be required to complete exhaustive enquiries by the court about the backgrounds and parenting capacities of parents in the form of a matrimonial proceedings report in disputed cases. This will be used by the sheriff, in conjunction with other information, to make decisions about the disputed custody of children.

In recent years 'access centres' have begun to be established where the non-custodial parent can visit comfortably with his/her children. This may help to alleviate what many experience as the most stressful part of the experience of access, which is the collection of the child from the custodial parent in what generally had been the matrimonial home.

(7) Cohabitation

In general, simple cohabitation will create no legal relationship between the parties and will have few legal consequences. The principal effects to note will be possible effects on any benefit claimed, and the entitlement of cohabitees to apply for occupancy rights under the Matrimonial Homes (Family Protection)(Scotland) Act 1981.

(8) Implications of demographic changes for social workers

Recent statistics[1] indicate that divorce rates have doubled since 1971 and that nearly four in ten marriages contracted in the 1980s are likely to break down. One in four children will experience the process of his/her parents' divorce by the time he/she is 16. One marriage in three will end in divorce by the time the spouses are 45. The figures suggest it is increasingly likely that social workers will have contact with families affected by these changes. Research[2] highlights the probability that parents are least able to cope with the demands being made upon them especially with regard to their children during the

1 See for example DSS Research Report No 6 *Lone Parent Families in the UK* by J Bradshaw & J Millar (1991).
2 See for example *Second Chances* by J Wallerstein and S Blakeslee (1989).

process of divorce and so most in need of advice, guidance and support which a social worker may be well placed to provide.

In April 1990 a rule of court allowed the court hearing a divorce application to refer the parties to a conciliation service for assistance in reaching agreements. Agreed decisions can be reached regarding for example custody, access, education of the children, the outline of disposition of the matrimonial home and other financial matters (which must then be referred back to solicitors[1]), and other pending matters outwith the court's adversarial procedure.

3. ADOPTION

(1) Introduction

Adoption is a process by which a new legal relationship of parent and child is created by transferring the parental rights of the child's original parent(s) to adoptive parent(s). In broad terms, as far as the law is concerned, the relationship between the child and the adoptive parent(s) is the same as that with his/her original parent(s). The effect of an adoption order therefore is to sever the legal relationship between the child and his/her original parent(s). An adoption order therefore terminates rights of access and also terminates a parental rights resolution. Adoption is now governed by the Adoption (Scotland) Act 1978.

About half of all adoptions are what are described as related adoptions, in other words at least one of the adoptive parents is related to the child, usually the child's mother. Although it may seem rather curious that a mother, who already has parental rights, would want to adopt her child, this is necessary under the current legal framework. The most usual situation is that the mother wants to adopt the child with a new partner. If the partner alone adopted the child he would acquire parental rights over the child, and, as we have noted above, the rights of the mother would be extinguished: thus the mother must adopt along with the new partner to retain parental rights and a legal relationship with the child.

The other half of adoptions are arranged by adoption agencies. All regional and islands councils are adoption agencies, and there are a number of independent adoption societies approved as adoption agencies by the Secretary of State.

1 See Code of Practice agreed with the Law Society of Scotland.

Slightly different rules apply to related adoptions and those arranged by an adoption agency. These differences will be considered as appropriate.

One of the main differences is that adoption agencies must appoint an adoption panel. The function of the adoption panel is to make recommendations to the agency as to the suitability of prospective adopters, the suitability of a particular adoption placement, and about whether adoption or freeing for adoption is in the child's best interests. The agency must take the views of the panel into account before reaching any of these decisions. The composition of these panels is not dissimilar to that of the fostering panels[1].

(2) Who can adopt?

There are certain age restrictions affecting the ability to adopt. If a married couple wishes to adopt then both partners must be 21 years of age, unless one is the child's parent, in which case he/she need only be 18. A single individual wishing to adopt must be at least 21. In the case of single individuals there are further restrictions:

(a) If married, he/she can only adopt once separated, if the other spouse cannot be found, or if the other spouse is, for health reasons, incapable of making application.
(b) If he/she is the father/mother of the child the other natural parent must be dead, have disappeared, or there must be some reason justifying his/her exclusion.

Adoptive parents for children placed by an adoption agency must be approved by the agency. The process of approval involves a lengthy and detailed investigation of the prospective adopters, their family circumstances and their motives for wishing to adopt. As in the process of investigation to become foster parents[2], the investigation by the social worker is likely to be protracted over a period of months and to be informed by guidelines from British Agencies for Adoption and Fostering. On completion of this investigation a report is produced which will then be considered by the Adoption Panel who will advise on the suitability of the prospective adopters. The agency will then decide whether or not they are suitable.

Aside from the above there are no **legal** restrictions on ability to adopt. Agencies may, however, impose restrictions as a matter of

1 See ch 4, pt 7(2).
2 See ch 4, pt 7(2).

policy. They may, for example, refuse to allow people over a certain age to adopt babies; some of these restrictions have been criticised as arbitrary and discriminatory.

(3) Who can be adopted?

Anyone under the age of 18 who is not and has never been married can be adopted. There are however certain requirements as to residence with the proposed adopters before an adoption order can be granted. These are:

(a) Where the prospective adopter is the child's parent, step-parent or a relative or where the placement has been made by an adoption agency the child must have had a home with the adopters for at least 13 weeks prior to the adoption and be at least 19 weeks old.
(b) In other cases the child must have had a home with the adopters for 12 months.

In addition the court must be satisfied before making the order that the local authority (where the placement is not by an adoption agency) or adoption agency has had sufficient opportunity to see the child with the adopters in their home environment. This requirement may prolong the periods set out above.

Children aged 12 or over must consent to the adoption and their consent can only be dispensed with if they are incapable of giving it. In addition the court is required to ascertain, having regard to the age and understanding of the child, his/her wishes and feelings regarding the proposed adoption and to give due consideration to these in making the decision. The wishes of children under the age of 12 are therefore also relevant.

(4) Rights of the child's parents

The parents in this instance are the legal parents of the child as defined above. The parents must consent to the adoption, but there is provision for that consent to be dispensed with in the following cases:

(a) If the parent cannot be found or is incapable of giving consent;
(b) if the parent is withholding consent unreasonably. This decision will be taken by the sheriff in light of all the circumstances of a case;

(c) if the parent has persistently failed without reasonable cause to discharge his/her parental duties;
(d) if the parent has abandoned or neglected the child;
(e) if the parent has persistently mistreated the child;
(f) if the parent has seriously mistreated the child.

The consent of the child's mother to adoption (or to freeing for adoption) is ineffective if it is granted within six weeks of the birth of the child.

(5) Freeing for adoption

At a stage before the application for an adoption order is made an adoption agency may apply for an order freeing a child for adoption. If parental agreement to this is to be dispensed with the child must already have been placed for adoption or be likely to be placed for adoption. The effect of a freeing order is that parental rights (including the right to consent to adoption) and duties are vested in the adoption agency. The child's parent can apply to have a freeing order revoked.

(6) Placement with proposed adopters

Where the placement is arranged by the adoption agency any placement of a child with possible adopters must be considered by the adoption panel, and the advice of the panel taken into account.

(7) Adoption procedure

The main feature of the adoption process in court is the emphasis on confidentiality. There are strict limits on those allowed to see the court papers which must be sealed at the end of the case. Any court hearings must be held in private unless the court directs otherwise (this is unlikely).

If the child has not been placed for adoption by an adoption agency the local authority must be informed of the intention to adopt. Before an adoption order can be granted a report must then be produced by the local authority. The report will cover such matters as the suitability of the applicant and any matters relevant to the effect of the adoption on the safeguarding and promotion of the child's welfare; relevant matters would include the occupations of the adopters and their ability to look after the child. In addition the report must comment on the feelings and wishes of the child. Finally the report must confirm that the placement has not been made contrary to section 11 of the Adoption (Scotland) Act 1978, which only permits placements to be made by an adoption agency unless the proposed adopter is a relative of the child. Where the placement has been made by an adoption agency they must provide a report covering all of these matters.

Once the relevant reports have been obtained the petition for adoption can be lodged in court and in virtually all cases the court will be the sheriff court. Along with the petition the report mentioned above will be lodged, together with evidence as to the health of the proposed adopters.

Once the petition is lodged a *curator ad litem* and reporting officer will be appointed. In sheriff court cases these two posts will be combined unless this is not reasonably practicable. The individual appointed may be drawn from a panel maintained by the local authority, and if this is done and the adoption order is granted the authority will pay his/her fees.

The duty of the *curator ad litem* is to protect the interests of the child in the proceedings and he/she must produce a report to the court. The functions of the *curator* are dealt with at length in the court rules. Briefly, they are to protect the child's interests, to ascertain whether the facts stated in the petition are correct, to establish whether the adoption is likely to safeguard and promote the welfare of the child, and to establish the reasons for adoption.

Reporting officers' duties are principally to witness the parents' consent to the adoption and to ensure that they understand the effects of adoption.

Following receipt of the reports a statutory hearing will be held. This may simply be a formality ending with the granting of the petition. The court, however, may wish to clarify matters from the reports and may wish to interview the petitioners and any person making a report to the court. Finally, the child's parent may appear and object to the granting of the order and in such a case a proof hearing may be necessary to ascertain whether the consent of the parent can be dispensed with.

At the end of the proceedings a number of options are open to the court. In making their decision they must give first consideration to the need to safeguard and promote the welfare of the child throughout his/her childhood and must, so far as practicable ascertain the wishes and feelings of the child regarding the decision and give due consideration to them, having regard to the child's age and understanding. The options are:

(a) To refuse the order.
(b) To grant the order as sought.

(c) To grant an interim order giving custody to the petitioners for up to two years. This is in the nature of a probationary period at the end of which an additional report will be produced by the curator and the matter resolved. An interim order may be appropriate, for example, where the petitioners appear rather immature or where there is some other problem which may be overcome by the passing of time. Interim orders are very rare in practice.
(d) To grant the order subject to conditions. If open adoptions were to become more accepted a condition could be attached requiring access by the child's parent.
(e) To grant an order for custody rather than adoption. This can be done in cases where the court considers it more appropriate, and, in cases of related adoptions, where they consider that custody would better promote and safeguard the child's welfare, eg if it was thought desirable to continue access by the (other) parent in cases where otherwise family relationships might become skewed.
(f) To make an order placing the child under the supervision of, or in the care of, a local authority. This type of order can be made if there are exceptional circumstances justifying it. This and the previous type of order are very rare in practice.

Once an adoption order is made it will be recorded in the Adopted Children's Register.

(8) Protected children

Once notice of a proposed adoption is given to the local authority the child involved becomes a protected child. The local authority has a duty to visit protected children from time to time to satisfy themselves as to their welfare. In practice this is most likely to be once a month.

(9) Access to adoption records

As we have noted the making of an adoption order is recorded in the Adopted Children's Register. In addition the Registrar General must keep other registers and information linking the Adopted Children's Register with a child's original birth certificate. Once an adopted child reaches the age of 17 he/she is entitled to access to these records. On application the Registrar General must advise the child of the availability of counselling. Counselling is optional but if it is requested it will be provided by an adoption society if they made the original placement, otherwise it will be provided by the local authority for the area where the child resides.

4. MATRIMONIAL HOMES (FAMILY PROTECTION) (SCOTLAND) ACT 1981

The Matrimonial Homes (Family Protection)(Scotland) Act 1981 deals with two main topics: the property rights of spouses who do not own or are not the tenants of the house they share with their spouse, and the provision of greater protection to spouses suffering from domestic violence. In practice, although the legislation refers throughout to spouses, the principal beneficiaries and the most numerous applicants to court under its various provisions are women.

There are four provisions of the Act which are of particular relevance. These are the provisions relating to occupancy rights; exclusion orders; matrimonial interdicts; and the transfer of tenancies. Cohabiting couples also enjoy some of the benefits of the Act and their position is considered at the end.

(1) Occupancy rights

Under the previous law the only person with a legal right to occupy a home was the person who was the owner or tenant of the property, or who enjoyed some other permission from the owner to occupy it. The difficulty in this was that the ownership or tenancy of the family home was usually taken in the name of the husband alone, with the consequence that the wife had no legally recognised right of occupation. She could therefore be ejected from the family home and had no legal power to prevent this or to resume occupation after it had happened.

The Act remedies this. It does this by defining the spouse who is the owner or tenant of the family home (referred to in the Act as the matrimonial home) as an 'entitled spouse' and the other spouse as a 'non-entitled spouse', and by granting all non-entitled spouses what is referred to as an 'occupancy right' in the family home.

The precise content of this occupancy right depends on whether or not the non-entitled spouse is in occupation of the matrimonial home. If she is, the right is to remain in occupation and to have free access to the home. If not, the right is to be allowed to enter and occupy the matrimonial home. Should access be refused or should the non-entitled spouse be excluded from the home, the occupancy right can only be enforced by application to court. While this right is a considerable improvement over the previous situation, it is important to acknowledge and appreciate that the non-entitled spouse (usually the woman) may need support and assistance from a social worker or others to consider this as one alternative living situation, which may or may not be the preferred or most appropriate option.

The situation noted above where the title to the matrimonial home was in the name of only one of the spouses is now rarer. It is much commoner now for the title to be taken in the joint names of the husband and wife. Where this is the case both have property rights, including occupancy rights, in the home regardless of the 1981 Act.

Wherever occupancy rights exist either spouse can apply to court for an order enforcing the rights, restricting the occupancy rights of the other spouse, regulating the exercise of the other spouse's occupancy rights, or protecting the occupancy rights of the spouse applying for the order. Either spouse may also apply for an exclusion order barring the other from the matrimonial home.

(2) Exclusion orders

Either spouse can apply to court for an exclusion order suspending the occupancy rights of the other. This can be done **both** where there is an entitled and non-entitled spouse **and** where the title to the property is joint and both spouses are effectively entitled spouses. It is now clear that the spouse applying for the exclusion order need not be in occupation of the matrimonial home when the application is made.

There are two requirements to be fulfilled before the court can grant the order. Firstly, the order must be necessary to protect the applicant or any child of the family from actual or threatened conduct of the other spouse which would be detrimental to their physical or mental health. Secondly, the court must not make an order if it would be unjustified or unreasonable to do so.

(a) Need for protection. In the first place making the order must be necessary. The implication is that there must be no other remedy, for example an interdict, which will provide the necessary protection. On the other hand it does not mean that an applicant must proceed in stages; first of all seeking interdict and then, if that is unsuccessful, applying for an exclusion order.

The threat must come from some conduct on the part of the other spouse. The provision will therefore not cover the case where the upset arises simply from the other spouse's desire to remain in the matrimonial home despite the break-up of the relationship.

Finally it should be noted that actual physical injury need not have occurred for an order to be granted.

The courts have formulated four relevant questions to be considered in deciding on this type of application. They are:

(i) What is the nature and quality of the alleged conduct?

(ii) Is the court satisfied that the conduct is likely to be repeated if cohabitation continues?
(iii) Has the conduct been, or, if repeated would it be, injurious to the physical or mental health of the applicant spouse or any child of the family?
(iv) If so, is the order sought necessary for the future protection of the physical or mental health of the applicant or child?[1]

(b) Unjustified or unreasonable. In deciding on whether granting the order would be unjustified or unreasonable the Act directs the court to consider a number of factors. These include the conduct of the parties, the respective needs and resources of the parties, the needs of any children, and the offer by an entitled spouse to make accommodation available to the non-entitled spouse. In the specific case of tied housing where there is a requirement that the non-applicant spouse reside there, the courts must consider that requirement and the possible consequences of making an exclusion order in deciding whether or not it is unjustified or unreasonable to make the order.

When the court makes an exclusion order it must also, if requested to do so by the applicant, grant a warrant for the ejection of the other spouse from the home and/or an interdict preventing the other spouse from entering the matrimonial home without the permission of the spouse applying for the order. The court may also grant an interdict prohibiting the other spouse from entering or remaining in a specified area in the vicinity of the matrimonial home.

Pending the grant of a full exclusion order the court may make an interim (temporary) order, this may only be done if the non-applicant spouse has been afforded an opportunity of being heard or represented in court before the interim order is made.

(3) Transfer of tenancy

Where the matrimonial home is rented in the name of the entitled spouse only, the non-entitled spouse may apply to court for the tenancy to be transferred to her. Before granting such an order the court must consider all the circumstances of the case and in particular: the conduct of the spouses; the respective needs and resources of the spouses; the needs of any children; the extent of any business use of the home by one of the spouses; and any offer by the entitled spouse to provide accommodation for the non-entitled spouse.

1 *McCafferty v McCafferty* 1986 SLT 650.

(4) Matrimonial interdicts

In general terms an interdict is a court order requiring an individual to desist from a course of conduct which is causing or is likely to cause injury (whether physical, mental or financial) or detriment to another or interfere with his/her legal rights. Normally breach of the terms of an interdict is a civil matter and will only be punished if the person who has obtained the interdict takes proceedings to bring the offender before the court. If this is done the offender can be punished since he/she is guilty of contempt of court.

The 1981 Act, however, introduced a new category: matrimonial interdicts. A matrimonial interdict is one which either:

(a) Restrains or prohibits any conduct of one spouse towards the other spouse or towards a child of the family; or
(b) prohibits a spouse from entering or remaining in a matrimonial home or in a specified area in the vicinity of the home.

The peculiarity of a matrimonial interdict is that the court can attach to it a power of arrest which gives the police the power to arrest if there is reasonable cause to suspect that a breach of the interdict has taken place. A power of arrest **must** be attached where the interdict is associated with an exclusion order or interim exclusion order and the spouse applying for the interdict applies for the power of arrest to be attached. In other cases where the power of arrest is applied for, it **must** be attached to the interdict where the non-applicant spouse has had the opportunity of being heard or represented before the court, unless it appears to the court that in all the circumstances the power of arrest is unnecessary. A matrimonial interdict with a power of arrest attached must be notified to the non-applicant spouse and the Chief Constable.

The power of arrest is to the effect that a constable **may** arrest if breach of the interdict is suspected. The guidance issued to Chief Constables by the Lord Advocate is more explicit. It states that:

'[T]he presumption should be that the offending spouse will be arrested in all but the most trivial cases. In other words, the discretion not to arrest should be used sparingly and only for good reasons, bearing in mind that the safety of the applicant spouse is the paramount consideration.

Even in circumstances where the offending spouse has left the locus before the arrival of the police, the presumption should be in favour of pursuing him to effect an arrest unless there are compelling reasons to the contrary.'[1]

1 SCOLAG 122 (November 1986), 120.

Once the spouse has been arrested he may be freed if the officer in charge of the police station to which he is taken is satisfied that there is no likelihood of violence to the other spouse or any child of the family. If the offending spouse is freed a report will be made to the procurator fiscal, and he may be prosecuted for any criminal offence that has been committed. If no prosecution takes place the other spouse must be informed.

If the spouse is not freed a report is made to the fiscal who may prosecute the spouse for any offence committed. If no prosecution takes place a petition is presented to the court and if the sheriff is satisfied that there is a prima facie breach of interdict, that civil proceedings for breach will be taken by the other spouse, and that there is a substantial risk of violence against the other spouse or child of the family he/she may order further detention for up to two days.

Finally, although the only express provision and mention in the Act is in respect of interdicts prohibiting entry to the matrimonial home and its vicinity, there is no reason why the husband cannot be interdicted from harassing the wife at work or the wife and children at any other place. Such an interdict, because it relates to the conduct of one spouse towards the other or towards a child of the family, would be a matrimonial interdict and could have a power of arrest attached.

(5) **Cohabiting couples**

In the case of couples living together as if man and wife where one has a title to the shared home and the other does not, the non-entitled partner may apply to court for the grant of occupancy rights. This grant may be made for up to six months, but is renewable for further six month periods. Where such an order is in force or where both partners are 'entitled', the provisions of the 1981 Act in relation to occupancy rights, exclusion orders and matrimonial interdicts apply to cohabiting couples in much the same way as to married couples. Non-entitled partners in rented accommodation may also apply for the transfer of the tenancy.

5. PROPOSED CHANGES IN THE LAW

In May 1992 the Scottish Law Commission produced a *Report on Family Law*[1] which contained a large number of proposals for significant changes in the law.

1 HC (1992/93) no 4.

One of the main areas of change was that of parental rights. The Law Commission recommend that there should be a statutory statement of parental responsibilities with it being made clear that the rights parents have are given to them to allow them to fulfil their responsibilities. The responsibilities of parents would be to safeguard and promote the health, development and welfare of their children and to give them guidance and direction appropriate to their stage of development.

In addition parental rights of custody, access and guardianship would be replaced by a new set of rights, for example to have a child live with the parent until the age of 16 or to have contact with the child if not living with him/her. Custody and access orders would be replaced with residence and contact orders, with court orders dealing with other matters being referred to as specific issue orders. Parental rights would be conferred on both parents regardless of their marital status.

Other changes affecting children would be a right for them to have their views considered before any major decision affecting them was taken and a restriction on physical punishment.

Finally, a variety of other reforms relating to marriage, divorce, separation and the Matrimonial Homes (Family Protection)(Scotland) Act 1981 are proposed. These include the abolition of marriage by cohabitation with habit and repute and an extension of the rights of cohabiting couples allowing, for example, claims for financial provision on the termination of cohabitation.

4. Child care law

1. INTRODUCTION

There is no field in social work practice which has a higher public profile and which engenders more anxiety for all those involved than child care. Changing public attitudes and views about what characterises good enough parenting, the rights and responsibilities of parents, the rights of children, the justification for state intervention into family life, and the need to protect children have each contributed to the ongoing debate about the most appropriate role for social workers. The intricacies of the dynamic operating amongst the social work departments, the children's hearings and the courts further complicate an understanding of the duties and responsibilities of social workers. The social work departments have a duty to investigate complaints/allegations of child abuse of all descriptions[1]. Local authorities have established detailed procedures and guidelines for all aspects of this work including working with other professions. These procedures are being formalised and regularised through guidance from Social Work Services Group circulars which increasingly have focused on child protection.

'By statute social work departments have a primary responsibility for child care and for carrying out associated work on prevention, treatment and counselling. From this flows their management responsibility for dealing with child abuse, but it has many facets and is so sensitive that other public services and voluntary organisations inevitably have important parts to play in dealing with cases. Reporters and children's hearings are involved in deciding when compulsory measures of care are needed. The courts may be involved if an offence has been committed and in some cases a prison sentence may follow. In both situations reports, supervision and advice may be required from the social work department. The growing pressure on services has underlined the need for a well co-ordinated, interdisciplinary approach to child abuse which

1 See also pts 3, 4(2).

aims to secure the best interests of children and their families and at the same time ensures best use of available resources.'[1]

The Kilbrandon Committee's[2] core recommendations were accepted and used to form the basis for much of the Social Work (Scotland) Act 1968. The philosophy exemplified in these documents emphasised the promotion of social welfare, the lack of distinction between the needs of children either referred for having allegedly committed offences or against whom offences had allegedly been committed, and the treatment rather than punishment of children. Subsequent legislation, like the Children Act 1975, has been incorporated into the Social Work (Scotland) Act 1968 which has extended and amended its provisions but has not altered the essential nature of the statute.

When the Secretary of State announced in 1988 that a radical review of child care law in Scotland was not required and the Child Care Law Review Group was established with the limited remit of identifying 'options for change and improvement in child care law which would simplify and improve arrangements for protecting children at risk and caring for children and families in need' while assessing the resource implications for any proposed amendments to the law, Scotland once again diverged dramatically from developments in England and Wales which led to a fundamental overhaul and consolidation of child care law and eventually the implementation of the Children Act 1989.

The Child Care Law Review Group concluded that there may not be a need for drastic changes but it did make recommendations for significant changes which would bring the law 'up to the needs of children and families in Scotland in the 90s and beyond'.[3] The inquiry into the Orkney cases being conducted by Lord Clyde is also likely to produce recommendations for change.

2. CHILDREN IN NEED OF CARE

Children are received into the care of the local authority for an enormous range of reasons and through a number of very different statutes. The social workers', the child's and the parents' rights and responsibilities will vary considerably depending upon the route of the child into care and the prevailing statute. Social work depart-

1 From SWSG circular SW9/1988, para 2.
2 *Children and Young Persons* Cmnd 2306 (1964).
3 Scottish Office *Review of Child Care Law in Scotland* (1990) para 27.4.

ments' policies reflect the received wisdom that unless there is overwhelming evidence to suggest otherwise, the child's best interest is served by being at home with his/her family and so the preventive work which is the **duty** of the social work department (to 'diminish the need' to receive children into care or being referred to a children's hearing[1]) is a dominant feature of practice. The corollary is also reflected in practice; that it is normally the plan to enable children to be returned to the home of their parents at the earliest feasible point. The *Code of Practice: Access to Children in Care or Under Supervision in Scotland* issued by the Secretary of State in 1983 makes this expectation clear : 'For most children the aim must be to enable them to return to live with their families successfully in as short a time as possible'[2].

The (potential) reception of a child into the care of the local authority vies for being amongst the most stressful events in the lives of all concerned. The social worker's role in these situations can often be contradictory. At its crudest and simplest, there is often a conflict of interest amongst the child, the family and the local authority at the point of reception into care and the resulting tensions must be carefully managed. Social workers will be hard pressed to systemically assess, negotiate decision making and marshall appropriate resources while remaining open to the feelings of all those involved in the process, including themselves.

(1) Voluntary reception

This description is rather a misnomer as far as most children are concerned since the voluntary element refers to the fact that essentially the child remains in care only as long as the parent(s) wish him or her to, unless the local authority takes some form of action (although see the discussion of *M v Dumfries & Galloway Regional Council*[3] below). The legal basis for voluntary care is section 15 of the 1968 Act. This imposes a **duty** on local authorities to receive a child who **appears** to be under the age of 17 into care where the following two conditions are fulfilled:

(a) Either (i) the child has no parent or guardian, has been abandoned or is lost; or
(ii) the child's parent/guardian is prevented by some

1 Social Work (Scotland) Act 1968, s12(2)(a).
2 Paragraph 7.
3 1991 SCLR 481.

physical or mental incapacity or by some other circumstances from providing for the child's proper accommodation, maintenance or upbringing. This applies whether the inability to provide is permanent or temporary: and

(b) the intervention of the local authority is necessary in the interests of the child's welfare.

As noted above, voluntary reception will require the consent, or at least the acquiescence, of the child's parents if they can be found. In practice the parents are normally asked to sign a form consenting to the reception into care, as well as a consent to medical treatment for their children while in care (see below). Such receptions may, indeed, be initiated by a parent, for example, if a lone parent has to go into hospital for an operation and has no one else to look after the child-(ren). Most children received into care under section 15 remain in care for a brief period and then return to their parent(s) home to live.

The parents retain the right to remove their child from care at any time with the only statutory restriction being that if the child has been in care for more than six months the authority must either consent to removal or the parents must give 28 days notice of their intention to remove. The statutory provisions, then, appear to give the parents the absolute right to remove a child in care under section 15. If, however, the local authority refuses to let the parents remove the child the parents only recourse is to raise a court action to have the child delivered to them. This is what happened in the case of *M v Dumfries & Galloway Regional Council*. Here a child of 12 had been in care under section 15 for three years. Arrangements for the child's return home were well under way when she made allegations of sexual abuse against her father. Two months later the parents gave 28 days notice of their intention to remove the child from care, the regional council refused to deliver the child, and the parents raised a court action seeking an order requiring the council to deliver the child. The sheriff decided that the application was an application relating to parental rights in terms of section 3 of the Law Reform (Parent and Child)(Scotland) Act 1986[1], and as such the court had to be satisfied that granting the order was in the best interests of the child. The sheriff decided that it was not and refused the order.

The consequence of this case is that it now appears that local authorities are within their rights to refuse to return a child in care

1 See ch 3, pt 1(6).

under section 15 where it would not be in the child's best interests. There are dangers and problems in local authorities making use of this decision to keep children in care. The local authority may fail to convince the court about the child's best interests and may, as a result, irreparably damage relationships with the parents. More fundamentally this means of taking a child into compulsory care avoids the safeguards for parents and children which are brought into play if other procedures for taking a child into compulsory care are used.

Once a child has been received into care under section 15 the local authority has an obligation to care for him/her until the age of 18. They are obliged, where the whereabouts of the child's parents are unknown, to try to find them, and, where this would be consistent with the interests of the child, to seek to have his/her care taken over by his/her parent/guardian or a relative or friend.

(2) Assumption of parental rights

Section 16 of the 1968 Act gives local authorities the power to take over and exercise parental rights in respect of children in their care. Social workers, their child care advisors and their managers take decisions about pursuing parental rights resolutions. They prepare reports and on the advice of local authority legal advisors, a precis of this material is presented to the social work (sub) committee of the local authority who either pass or reject this resolution. This is not a process which is open to public scrutiny although it is performed by elected representatives, and so some have argued that it is undemocratic and open to abuse.

Before the local authority can pass a resolution (referred to as a parental rights resolution) the child must be in their care under section 15 or under some other statutory provision, including a child subject to a supervision order under either section 44(1)(a) or section 44(1)(b); secondly, the assumption of parental rights must be necessary for the welfare of the child; and, finally, one of the grounds specified in section 16 must exist in relation to the child or his/her parents. Where a child has two parents with parental rights the assumption of parental rights may involve taking over the parental rights of only one of them.

(a) *Grounds for assumption of parental rights*

(i) The child's parents are dead and the child has no legal guardian. Where the parents are dead a guardian can be appointed by the court or may have been appointed in the parent's will.

(ii) The parent/guardian whose rights are being assumed **either**

(a) has abandoned the child. Aside from any other circumstances the 1968 Act provides that a child is to be regarded as having been abandoned if the parent/guardian has been unknown to the local authority for a period of 12 months during which the child has been in care; or

(b) suffers from some permanent disability which makes him/her incapable of caring for the child. This could be an illness or some physical condition; or

(c) suffers from a mental illness or deficiency making him/her unfit to have care of the child; or

(d) is of such habits or mode of life as to be unfit to have the care of the child. Examples of habits or modes of life which would fall within this category are alcoholism, indulging in prostitution and being addicted to drugs. Reported cases have involved people with an unsettled way of life who change accommodation frequently and couples who separate regularly, usually in acrimonious circumstances. The mode or way of life referred to need not be morally reprehensible or voluntarily undertaken, eg it has been suggested that this category would include religious hermits and long term prisoners.

For this ground to exist the parent(s) need never have had physical care of the child, all that is relevant is his/her way of life and that it makes him/her unfit to have care of the child. In the case of *Lothian Regional Council v T*[1] a parental rights resolution passed on a 16 month old child who had never been cared for by the parents, having been placed in foster care direct from the maternity hospital, was upheld. In this case the court was satisfied on the evidence of the parents' lack of a settled home and unstable relationship that they were unfit to have the care of the child; or

(e) has so persistently failed without reasonable cause to fulfil the obligations of a parent/guardian as to be unfit to have care of the child. Two things must be established. First, a failure to discharge parental obligations. This failure need not be intentional on the part of the parent, all that is necessary is to establish that it has happened on a number of occasions. Second, that there was no reasonable cause for the failure. This question is approached from the point of view of an objective standard, ie asking how a reasonable parent would behave, rather than considering whether in the context of the individual parent the

1 1984 SLT 74.

failure is reasonable or justifiable[1]. Examples would include failure to supervise children properly or neglect of their hygiene.

(iii) A parent in respect of whom a parental rights resolution has been passed is, or is about to become, a member of the same household as the child and the other parent.

(iv) The child has been in the care of the local authority for more than three years.

(b) Procedure

The process of assumption of parental rights will be initiated by a decision of the social work department that assumption of parental rights is necessary in the interests of the child and that grounds under section 16 exist. Social Work Services Group circular SW4/1984 sets out guidelines to be followed before this decision is made. These guidelines include a reminder about section 20 (ie that in taking any decision about a child in care the welfare of the child is paramount and the child's wishes must be taken into account) and stress the importance of involving the child's parents.

Once a decision has been taken that assumption of parental rights is necessary, a recommendation is made to the social work committee of the regional or islands council, and it is that committee, or, more probably, a sub-committee, that will decide whether or not to assume parental rights. If the committee passes a parental rights resolution, that has the effect, unless challenged by the parent(s), of transferring parental rights to the local authority.

Once a resolution is passed the parents must be notified forthwith[2]. The parent has the right to serve a counter-notice on the local authority within one month of receipt of notification of the resolution. If the local authority does not apply to the sheriff court for an order confirming the resolution within 14 days of the receipt of the counter-notice the resolution will lapse. Legal aid is available to parents in such actions.

On application by the local authority the sheriff can confirm the resolution or refuse the application. Before the resolution can be confirmed the sheriff must be satisfied on the following three points:

(i) That confirmation is in the best interests of the child.

(ii) That grounds under section 16 were made out (ie established) at the time the resolution was passed.

1 See *Central Regional Council v B* 1985 SLT 413 for a fuller discussion.

2 A term sufficiently flexible to allow notification one month after the decision; see *Dumfries & Galloway Regional Council v M* 1990 SLT 272.

(iii) That at the time of the court hearing there continue to begrounds which would justify the passing of a resolution. These grounds need not be the same grounds as existed at the time the resolution was passed, and it is possible that because of delays in the court system ground (iv) above may be established in the course of proceedings but after the resolution was passed[1]. The court must still, however, be satisfied that confirming the resolution is in the best interests of the child.

(c) *Effect of parental rights resolution*

The effect of a parental rights resolution is that the local authority takes over, with four exceptions, the rights which a parent would normally have in respect of his/her child and which have been discussed above.

The four exceptions are:

(i) The authority cannot change the child's religious persuasion.
(ii) The parents remain liable to support the child financially.
(iii) The consent of the parents must be obtained for any adoption or application to free for adoption.
(iv) The parents retain a right of access to the child.

A parental rights resolution, unless rescinded, lasts until the child is 18. It may be rescinded at any time by the local authority, or the parent may apply to the sheriff court to have the resolution discontinued. The sheriff may discontinue the resolution if satisfied that there was no ground for passing the resolution or that it is in the interests of the child to have the resolution discontinued. In any application of this nature the sheriff may, instead of granting the application, order the authority to allow the care of the child to be taken over by the applicant.

During the life of the parental rights resolution the parents may wish to challenge decisions taken by the authority. There are two ways in which this might be done. First, in appropriate cases, by seeking judicial review of decisions or actions taken by the authority. Secondly, section 3 of the Law Reform (Parent and Child)(Scotland) Act 1986 would seem to make it possible to challenge the authority's decisions in the sheriff court and on a wider basis.

In line with the generally accepted desirability of maintaining contact with parent(s) and/or rehabilitating the child with the parents, the authority may place the child with his/her parents or a friend where this would appear to be beneficial to the child.

1 *Central Regional Council v B* 1985 SLT 413.

(d) *Rights of access*

Until 1984 parents who had been the subject of a parental rights resolution had no statutory right of access to the child concerned, although the code of practice issued by the Secretary of State does emphasise the desirability of maintaining links between the child and parents. Since then parents who have had access refused or terminated have had a right to apply to the sheriff court for an order granting access (known as an access order). The authority must now give formal notice of refusal or termination of access.

Once an access order has been made it can only be varied by further application to the sheriff. Where there is a danger that continued access in accordance with the order would put the child at serious risk the local authority can apply to the sheriff. The sheriff may then suspend the access order provided he/she is satisfied that serious risk of harm to the child exists. The suspension lasts initially for seven days, but if, during that period, the authority makes an application to vary the access order the suspension will be effective until that application is disposed of.

In making any decision on access orders the sheriff must have as the first and paramount consideration the welfare of the child. Local authorities, as well as considering this, must also have regard to the Code of Practice which emphasises that a high priority is to be placed on arranging and maintaining close links between the child in care and his or her family. In most cases access arrangements will be central in the planning for children to be returning home to live. Social worker's adherence to the ideals of rehabilitation of the family requires careful assessment and balancing of the needs of children and of parents for the maintenance and sustenance of relationships.

Temporary postponement of access for a reasonable time to allow for proper consideration of the arrangements to be made does not count as refusal of access giving rise to a right to apply to the sheriff.

More significantly the right to apply for an access order does not arise where access arrangements not regulated by an access order are altered, even where the effect of the alteration is a severe restriction of the right of access. In one case the sheriff principal expressed dissatisfaction with this state of affairs and gave as one of the reasons for refusing to confirm a parental rights resolution the fact that it might have the effect of seriously restricting parental access which, in his view, would not be in the child's interests[1].

1 *Lothian Regional Council v S* 1986 SLT (Sh Ct) 37.

(e) Vesting of parental rights in voluntary organisations

The local authority may, instead of assuming parental rights themselves, vest them, by means of a parental rights resolution, in a voluntary organisation. The provisions outlined above all apply to such a resolution and, additionally, there is the power for the authority to remove the rights from the voluntary organisation and assume them itself where this appears necessary in the interests of the child's welfare.

3. PLACE OF SAFETY ORDERS

A place of safety order provides a means for removing a child at risk to a place of safety[1]. Social workers and their managers take decisions about children believed to be at such a degree of risk that they must urgently be removed from the care of their parent(s). The power to intervene so intrusively in the private lives of families is the subject of much debate and misunderstanding. The quality of the information processing, decision-making and the interaction skills of the social workers will contribute toward a child being compulsorily removed from parent(s) in a manner which is conducive to future work towards either the child's return home or placement in a permanent alternative. The unresolved societal conflicts about the role of social workers are perhaps most clearly seen in the use of place of safety orders.

More specifically place of safety orders allow any person (eg a social worker) authorised by a justice of the peace (JP) or sheriff to remove a child to a place of safety. In terms of the 1968 Act a place of safety is any residential or other establishment provided by a local authority; a police station; or any hospital, surgery or other suitable place in which the occupier is willing to receive a child on a temporary basis.

Before a place of safety order can be obtained one or more of the grounds stated in section 37(2) of the 1968 Act must be present (though the extent to which JPs investigate the grounds in practice is unclear). A police constable, provided these grounds are fulfilled, can take a child to a place of safety without first obtaining an order. The grounds are:

(a) One of the offences listed in Schedule 1 of the Criminal Procedure (Scotland) Act 1975 has been or is believed to have been committed in respect of the child. A list of Schedule 1 offences forms

1 Section 37 of the 1968 Act.

an appendix to this chapter. But in general they cover neglect of children, violence towards children and sexual offences involving children.
(b) The child is a member of the same household as a child in respect of whom a Schedule 1 offence has been committed.
(c) The child is, or is likely to become, a member of the same household as someone who has committed a Schedule 1 offence.
(d) The child, being the child of a travelling person, is being prevented from receiving a proper education.
(e) The child is likely to be caused unnecessary suffering or serious impairment of health because of lack of parental care.

A place of safety order under section 37(2) only enables the social worker to take the child to a place of safety. It gives no power to enter premises forcibly to take the child away or to search for the child. If this is necessary a place of safety warrant under the Criminal Procedure (Scotland) Act 1975 should be applied for. Such a warrant can be granted by a JP if there is reasonable cause to suspect either that the child has been or is being assaulted, ill-treated or neglected in a manner likely to cause unnecessary suffering or injury to health, or that any Schedule 1 offence has been or is being committed in respect of the child.

Anyone may apply for a place of safety warrant, but it can only be enforced by the police officer named in it. The constable will normally be accompanied by the person applying for the warrant, unless the JP directs otherwise, and the JP may direct that he or she is accompanied by a doctor. Under a place of safety warrant the constable has the power to enter and search premises.

Once the child has been taken to a place of safety the case must be referred immediately to the reporter to the children's panel. The child must be released:

(a) If the reporter decides to proceed no further.
(b) After the day on which a children's hearing sits to consider the case unless the hearing or sheriff extends the period of detention as indicated below.
(c) After seven days.

The legal requirement is that if the case is to be referred to a hearing, one should be arranged to deal with the case on the first lawful day after detention if this is practicable. This is not always the case, but the hearing should be held as soon as possible. The hearing may issue a warrant to continue the detention for two 21-day periods to allow time to deal with the case. Such continuations may only be made if required in the interests of the child or to prevent absconding.

Two further extensions of detention for 21-day periods may be made (again by means of a warrant) by the sheriff on application by the reporter, taking the total possible period of detention to 84 days following first appearance at a hearing. Extensions may only be granted by the sheriff if they are necessary to allow time for the hearing to deal with the case and where continuation of detention is in the child's best interests. The courts will take a very broad view of what is in the interests of the child. This is discussed in *Humphries v S*[1] where continued detention of a child with a history of offending to prevent him committing further offences was regarded as being in his interests. In exceptional circumstances where a longer period of detention than that permitted by statute is needed for the disposal of the case, this may be authorised by the Court of Session[2].

Once a child detained on a place of safety order or warrant is referred to a hearing he/she becomes subject to the same procedures as any other child referred to a hearing.

Finally, it should be noted that taking a child into care on a place of safety order or warrant probably does not give the authority the right to have the child medically examined in the absence of parental consent, or, in the case of older children, the child's consent[3].

4. CHILDREN IN NEED OF COMPULSORY MEASURES OF CARE

(1) Introduction

The 1968 Act, following on from the report of the Kilbrandon Committee, introduced a new way of dealing with what are described as children in need of compulsory measures of care. This category covers all of the groups of children who would previously have been dealt with in different ways through the court system and whose behaviour the Kilbrandon Committee regarded as being symptomatic of some social or family dislocation. The Kilbrandon Committee concluded that:

'In terms of the treatment measures to be applied, the children appearing before the courts, whatever the precise circumstances in which they do so, show a basic similarity of underlying situation. The distinguishing factor is

1 1986 SLT 683.
2 *Ferguson v P* 1989 SLT 681.
3 See also pt 6(5) below.

their common need for special measures of education and training, the normal upbringing process for whatever reason having failed or fallen short.'[1]

These children are now dealt with by way of referral to the reporter to the children's hearing who, after an initial investigation, decides whether or not the case should go on to a hearing. The courts are only involved in cases where there is a dispute about the grounds for taking action in respect of a child and as the forum for dealing with appeals against decisions of the hearing. In law anyone can refer a case to the reporter if they are of the view that a child may be in need of compulsory measures of care, so that, for example, a concerned neighbour could report suspicions of child abuse. In practice, however, most referrals (about two-thirds) come from the police, followed by the social work department, the procurator fiscal and educational sources.

Once a child has been referred to the reporter then he/she must carry out an initial investigation to decide how to proceed with the case. At this stage the reporter will seek information from a number of sources, including the social work department.

On completion of the investigation the reporter has three options. First, to take no further action. This happens in about half of all cases referred to the reporter. Examples of this include when there is insufficient evidence, when the child is already subject to a supervision requirement, or when compulsory care is believed to be unnecessary. Second, the case may be referred to the local authority for voluntary social work assistance, or, in the case of offences to the police/juvenile liaison officer. Finally, where the reporter is satisfied that the child may be in need of compulsory measures of care he/she can refer the case to a children's hearing.

The hearing which is convened to deal with the case of a child referred to a children's hearing will consist of three lay members drawn from the larger children's panel. These panel lists are maintained for each regional and islands authority. At least one of the members of the hearing must be a woman, and one of the members will act as chair.

(2) Obligations of the social work department

The social work department has a number of functions and obligations in connection with the operation of the children's hearing system. The first of these arises where they receive information sug-

1 *Children and Young Persons* Cmnd 2306 (1964), para 252.

gesting that a child may need compulsory measures of care. On receipt of that information the department should carry out enquiries, unless satisfied that this is unnecessary, and if satisfied that the child is in need of compulsory measures of care the department must pass on the information they have to the reporter. Secondly, the social work department has an obligation to provide reports on children who have been referred to a hearing. Finally, the department has a number of responsibilities in terms of providing supervision for children when this is required by a hearing, and for carrying out reviews of the cases of children subject to supervision requirements.

The production of a report for a child referred to a hearing (normally referred to as a social background report) can give rise to both opportunities and problems for the social worker. If the child and/or family are known to the social worker or social work department, then more comprehensive material may be available in the compilation of the report. The social worker is well placed to provide information about the children's hearing system, procedures and possible outcomes to the child and family while also collecting and analysing data about the people and situations involved. The report is to be completed before the hearing and the child/ family may not accept the grounds of referral and may be unwilling to participate in the preparation of a report. In such cases they cannot be forced to assist, though the social worker may try to persuade them that some level of co-operation is in their interest.

There may also be conflict over the identity of the client. Is it the hearing or is it the child and family with whom the worker may have to work if the child is placed on supervision? The legal answer is probably that the client is the hearing. This is reflected in the law's attitude to disclosure of the report to the child/family. The procedural rules for children's hearings provide that in the course of the hearing the chair 'shall inform the child and his parent of the substance of any reports, documents and information ... if it appears to him that this is material to the manner in which the case of the child should be disposed of and that its disclosure would not be detrimental to the interests of the child.'[1] The category of reports specifically includes social background reports. According to the Court of Session this rule makes it absolutely clear that reports and other documents should not be handed over to the child or his/her parents[2]. However, this only appears to prevent the physical handing over of reports by social workers, and says nothing about sharing the contents of the report, as

1 Children's Hearings (Scotland) Rules 1986, SI 1986/2291, para 19(3).
2 *Kennedy v A* 1986 SLT 358 at p362B.

appropriate in terms of professional judgement, with the child/ family. Moore's view that 'the disclosure by some social workers of their reports before the hearing is not considered good professional practice'[1] does not accord with what many practitioners would regard as being good practice grounded on mutuality and reciprocity.

(3) Grounds of referral

The grounds on which a child can be referred to a children's hearing, and which, if accepted or established, form the basis for any action taken by the hearing, reflect the variety of types of cases with which the Kilbrandon Report was concerned. The numbering adopted here reflects the numbering in subsection 32(2) of the 1968 Act.

(a) The child is beyond parental control.

(b) The child is falling into bad associations or exposed to moral danger.

Thomson suggests that this ground might exist where the child was associating with prostitutes, drug addicts, alcoholics or homosexuals[2]. One of the reported cases is of the father of the friend of a six-year-old girl shining a torch on her naked private parts.

(c) Lack of parental care is likely to cause the child unnecessary suffering or seriously impair the child's health or development.

It is sufficient for this ground to exist that lack of care is likely to occur based on the known habits of the carer(s); the child need never actually have been in their care[3].

The appropriate test for deciding whether lack of parental care is likely to cause these consequences is 'whether a reasonable person looking to the circumstances of the particular case would consider that the child is likely to be caused unnecessary suffering or serious impairment to her health and development through lack of parental care on the part of the mother.'[4] In this case failure by a mother to visit a child in hospital for five months was not sufficient to establish likely lack of care where the mother had serious medical problems and lived far from the hospital.

Lack of parental care may exist even where the parents act

1 G Moore *A Guide to the Children's Hearings*, p 34.
2 J Thomson *Family Law in Scotland* (2nd edn, 1991), p 243.
3 *McGregor v L* 1981 SLT 194.
4 *M v McGregor* 1982 SLT 41 at 43.

with the best of motives and even if the child appears to be well looked after. For example, this ground was held to be established in a case where the parents of a haemophiliac child were unwilling to give consent to treatment using Factor VIII, even though the court accepted that the parents were concerned parents and that their refusal to consent to this treatment arose from a fear that the child might become HIV positive as a result of the treatment[1]. Another example is a case where the children were described by the sheriff as well nourished and clean, but on two occasions they had effectively been thrown out of the house and left to fend for themselves. In both instances there were long delays before their absence was reported to the police by their father[2].

(d) Any of the offences specified in Schedule 1 to the Criminal Procedure (Scotland) Act 1975 has been committed in respect of the child or in respect of a child who is a member of the same household. A list of Schedule 1 offences forms an appendix to this chapter, but they include assaults on, neglect of, and sexual offences in relation to, children.

The identity of the offender need not be specified for this ground to exist or be established[3].

In relation to this ground and the two following, 'household' has an extended meaning and includes a family unit which would normally live together even though the individual members of the unit are temporarily separated. In *McGregor v H*[4] a child was referred to a hearing on the ground that she was a member of the same household as a child, her brother, who had been the victim of a Schedule 1 offence. The ground was held to be established even though her brother, who had been the victim of the offence, was separated from the rest of the family and living with foster parents.

Finally, it is worth noting that parents still have the right to use force on their children by way of punishment, provided that the force falls within the bounds of reasonable chastisement. Whether or not what a parent does falls within these boundaries will depend on the facts of each case, with the courts taking into account whether the parent lost his/her temper, the parent's intention, the blameworthiness of the child's conduct and the

1 *Finlayson, Applicant* 1989 SCLR 601.
2 *Kennedy v S* 1986 SLT 679.
3 *McGregor v K* 1982 SLT 293.
4 1983 SLT 626.

degree of force used[1]. Reasonable chastisement will not provide the grounds for a referral to a hearing under this subsection[2].

(dd) The child is, or is likely to become, a member of the same household as a person who has committed a Schedule 1 offence.

An example of this is where the father of the child referred to the hearing had committed the offence in relation to one of her friends.

(e) The child is a female and is a member of the same household as a female in respect of whom incest has been committed by a member of the household.

(f) The child has failed to attend school regularly without reasonable excuse.

A child suspended from school cannot be referred under this ground unless, possibly, the exclusion from school was made necessary by his/her behaviour[3].

(g) The child has committed an offence.

This follows from the provision that no child under the age of 16 is to be prosecuted except on the instructions of the Lord Advocate. If a child under 16 is prosecuted this may only be done in the High Court or in the sheriff court[4]. The offences which the Lord Advocate has instructed must be reported to the procurator fiscal for consideration for prosecution are:

(1) Serious offences which must be prosecuted on indictment. These include murder, rape, assault and robbery involving firearms, and fireraising causing considerable damage.

(2) Offences alleged to have been committed by children aged 15 or over where, in the event of conviction, disqualification from driving can be part of the penalty.

(3) Children over 16 but still under supervision can be referred to the procurator fiscal for prosecution.

This ground of referral is only available in respect of children over the age of eight, which is the age of criminal responsibility in Scots law[5].

(gg) The child has deliberately inhaled a volatile substance, other than for medicinal purposes, ie solvent abuse.

1 See *Stewart v Thain* 1981 SLT (Notes) 2; *Peebles v Macphail* 1990 SLT 245; *B v Harris* 1990 SLT 208; and *Byrd v Wither* 1991 SLT 206 for recent cases on this area of law.

2 *B v Harris, supra*.

3 *D v Kennedy* 1987 SLT 55.

4 See ch 6, pt 2(5).

5 *Merrin v S* 1987 SLT 193.

(h) The child has been referred under Part V of the 1968 Act. This covers children who have absconded or are subject to transfer within the United Kingdom.

(i) The child is in the care of the local authority and his/her behaviour is such that special measures are needed to ensure his/her adequate care and control.

This would cover the case of a child already in care whom it was felt to be appropriate to place in secure accommodation[1].

(4) Attendance and representation at hearings

Subject to the exceptions noted below the child concerned and his or her parents or guardians have a right, and are legally obliged, to attend the hearing. If the hearing is satisfied that requiring the attendance of the child's parents or guardians would be unreasonable or is unnecessary that attendance can be dispensed with. 'Parents' in this context means the same as those having parental rights and it is specifically provided that in the case where the mother and father of a child are not married 'parent' means the mother to the exclusion of the father. In such cases the father may, however, have a right to attend if he qualifies as a guardian, ie someone who in the opinion of the hearing has custody or charge of or actual control over the child[2]. Whether a father in such circumstances qualifies as a guardian has to be decided by the hearing in light of all the facts of the case[3].

If a child fails to appear, a warrant for his/her apprehension may be issued by the hearing and once detained the child should be brought before a hearing immediately, or, where this is impossible, on the first lawful day after apprehension.

The hearing does, however, have the power to consider a case, in whole or in part, without the child's attendance. This can be done either where the referral relates to a Schedule 1 offence and the hearing considers that the attendance of the child is not necessary for the just hearing of the case, or where they are satisfied that it would be detrimental to the interest of the child to be present at the hearing[4]. Unfortunately this appears to conflict with a later provision that before proceeding to consider a case the grounds of referral must be explained to the child[5]. This apparent conflict was discussed in *B v*

1 See below, pt 6(4).
2 Section 94(1).
3 *C v Kennedy* 1991 SCLR 167.
4 Section 40(2).
5 Section 42(1).

Sloan[1] where the Inner House of the Court of Session took the view that attendance could be dispensed with where this would not prejudice the child's rights, particularly the child's right to reject the grounds of referral and have them tested in an application to the sheriff court for a finding that the grounds are established.

The parents and child may be represented at the hearing, though it should be noted that the legal aid scheme does not cover the cost of legal representation at hearings, and representation is not common. In addition the chair may appoint a safeguarder to safeguard the child's interests where this appears to be necessary because of an actual or possible conflict of interest between the child and his/her parents[2]. The safeguarder will be selected from a panel maintained by the local authority. Most safeguarders are solicitors or have a qualification in social work.

The social worker who prepared the social background report will normally be in attendance at the hearing. He/she will make a choice about appropriate roles based on the assessment of the family and the situation. Sometimes this will highlight the contradictory expectations for the social worker mentioned earlier concerning who is the client and whose needs take precedence. It may be appropriate for the social worker to act as one who enables the full participation of the child and parent(s) in the hearing, in clarifying and updating the contents of the social background report, or even exceptionally in advocating on behalf of the child and/or parent(s) who may be disadvantaged by unfamiliarity with the system and/or the unequal power balance.

(5) **Procedure**

It is now clear that it is permissible for the hearing to have preliminary meetings in the absence of the child and his/her parents[3]. Such preliminary meetings might consider, for example, whether to dispense with the child's attendance or the parent's attendance.

The hearing itself should be conducted in private, and the number in attendance kept to a minimum. Generally speaking those in attendance will be the three panel members, the reporter, the child and parent(s), and the social worker who compiled the social background report.

The chair starts by explaining the grounds of referral to the parents

1 1991 SLT 530.
2 Section 34A.
3 *B v Sloan*, supra.

and the child (if present) and finding out if the grounds are accepted by the parents and child. If the grounds are accepted the hearing can proceed except where the child, for example because of age, is not capable of understanding or does not understand the explanation of the grounds. Where this is the case the hearing must either discharge the referral or instruct the reporter to apply to the sheriff for a finding that the grounds are established.

If the grounds are accepted in part, the hearing can proceed in respect of the grounds accepted. If the grounds are not accepted the hearing can discharge the referral or instruct the reporter to apply to the sheriff for a finding that the grounds are established.

Once the grounds have been accepted or established the hearing takes the form, in theory, of a round table discussion of the grounds, the reasons behind them, and future prospects.

After discussion the hearing must decide what course of action open to them is in the best interests of the child. This decision will be made in the presence of the child and his/her parents. The options available are:

(1) To take no further action and discharge the referral.
(2) To continue the referral for further investigation. As part of this the child may be required to attend or reside at an establishment such as a residential assessment centre, a hospital or clinic for the purposes of assessment.
(3) To make a supervision requirement. These are considered more fully below.

Whatever decision the hearing makes it must be communicated to the child and parents, and clear and comprehensible reasons must be given for the decision[1]. It may sometimes be appropriate for the social worker to spend time with the child and family following the panel's decision to clarify what the meaning of the decision is, to discuss the practicalities, and to make arrangements for future contacts. Hearings can be fraught with tension and may even contribute toward the precipitation of a crisis in the family and so the intervention of a social worker may be welcomed and necessary.

If a hearing is unable to dispose of a case (eg because the grounds of referral are disputed) it can issue a warrant for the detention of the child for up to 21 days. It can only do this if either:

(a) It is satisfied that detention is in the child's best interests; or
(b) it has reason to believe that the child may not attend any future

1 See *K v Finlayson* 1974 SLT (Sh Ct) 51.

hearing or other proceedings arising from the case (eg a hearing before the sheriff), or may fail to comply with a requirement to attend or reside at an establishment for the purposes of assessment.

This initial detention can be extended for a further 21 days by the hearing. Two further extensions, each for 21 days, may be made by the sheriff provided that he/she is satisfied that this is in the child's own interests. Application for extension by the sheriff will be made by the Reporter where it appears that the hearing will not be able to dispose of the child's case before the expiry of the current detention and where further detention is in the interests of the child[1].

(6) Application for finding that grounds are established

The application must be made within 28 days of the hearing and will be heard by the sheriff in chambers. The press are entitled to be present although the social worker is not. The parent(s) and child may apply for legal aid and are entitled to be legally represented. The sheriff may also, if this has not been done by the children's hearing, appoint a safeguarder to protect the child's interests. Any safeguarder appointed by the hearing will continue through the court hearing. The safeguarder must make a report to the court if he/she does not intend to appear at the court hearing, and may make a report in other circumstances. The report may contain recommendations[2].

After hearing evidence and considering the terms of any safeguarder's report, the sheriff may find the grounds not established and discharge the referral. Alternatively, the sheriff may find the grounds established and the matter will be referred back to the hearing for consideration and disposal. In order to find ground (g) above established the sheriff must be satisfied beyond reasonable doubt that the child has committed a crime, in other cases the sheriff must simply be satisfied that the ground is established on the balance of probabilities[3].

Where the ground of referral is that a Schedule 1 offence has been committed by a named individual, the court hearing on establishing the ground of referral should not, unless there are exceptional circumstances, be adjourned pending the outcome of any criminal trial[4].

1 1968 Act, s40.
2 *Kennedy v M* 1989 SLT 687.
3 1968 Act, s42(6). See *B v Kennedy* 1987 SLT 765; *Harris v F* 1991 SLT 242. See also ch 1, pts 9(5), 10(4).
4 *Ferguson v P* 1989 SLT 681.

Indeed even an acquittal of a Schedule 1 offence in criminal proceedings does not indicate that a supervision order made on the basis that the offence was established as a ground of referral should automatically be terminated[1].

It is also now clear that the sheriff should not, in most cases, rule on any procedural objections without hearing the evidence first. The only exceptions are where the objections, if successful, would mean that the grounds of referral could never be established[2]. An example of this would be a case where the referral was of a child under eight accused of an offence.

If the parents and child accept any of the grounds at a stage before the sheriff can make a finding the sheriff may find those grounds established without hearing further evidence regarding them.

If grounds of referral are established and the case referred back to the hearing for disposal the sheriff may issue a warrant for the child's detention if it is likely that he/she would run away before the hearing or if detention is in the child's own interests (eg if the ground of referral was commission of a Schedule 1 offence against the child). Such detention may last, at most, three days.

(7) Supervision requirements

Supervision requirements take two forms. The first of these, under section 44(1)(a), simply requires the child to submit to supervision by the social work department on whatever conditions the hearing may specify. These may include attendance at an intermediate treatment groupwork programme, attendance at a local resource centre, or other suitable resource. Although sometimes referred to as a home supervision order, this may, in fact, require the child to live with foster parents or at some other address away from home like a residential school for children with behavioural or learning disorders (formerly List 'G' schools). A requirement involving residence with foster parents can only be made if the hearing has received a report indicating the suitability of fostering and that the checks necessary before placing a child in foster care have been carried out[3]. A social worker may only recommend a fostering placement in the social background report if these checks have been carried out.

The second type of requirement, under section 44(1)(b), requires the child to stay in a residential establishment subject to whatever

1 *Kennedy v DB and DB* 1991 GWD 25–1421.
2 *B v Sloan*, 1991 SLT 530.
3 See below, pt 7(2).

other conditions the hearing may impose. The social work department can only make a recommendation that a child be placed in residential accommodation if they have completed either the procedure noted below in respect of placing children who have been in care more than six weeks in residential accommodation, or that for children in care less than six weeks, provided that they have also obtained certain additional information relating to the child and his/her family[1]. In both cases the recommendation can only be made if it is in the child's best interests. Many social work departments have adopted procedures which will not permit the social worker to recommend a residential order in his/her report without the agreement of a committee of more senior workers known sometimes as area resource groups or admissions and support units. The social worker's assessment as to the child's situation and needs will guide the decisions concerning the appropriateness of a residential order and permit matching with suitable resources.

Once a residential supervision requirement has been made the local authority must arrange for the child's reception into the named establishment. If it appears to them that the social work department will be unable to do this within 21 days of the making of the requirement the child's case must be referred to the reporter so that a further hearing can be arranged[2].

A residential supervision requirement may include a requirement that the child is to be placed in secure accommodation, providing conditions as to likelihood of absconding or injury to self or others are fulfilled[3]. Once such a requirement is made the child is to be kept in secure accommodation only at such times as the person in charge of the accommodation, with the agreement of the director of social work, considers necessary to give effect to the supervision requirement. This may mean that the child is never placed in secure accommodation.

In both types of supervision requirement the hearing can impose conditions regulating, or even preventing, parental access. Where conditions relating to access are imposed by a hearing, courts will not interfere with them. Any conditions attached to a supervision requirement must be clear and precise[4].

Once any supervision requirement has been made the child is

1 See below, pt 6(2).
2 Reporters Duties and Transmission of Information etc (Scotland) Rules 1971 (SI 1975/525), Rule 12.
3 See pt 6(4), where these conditions are explained more fully.
4 *D v Strathclyde Regional Council* 1991 SCLR 185.

regarded as being in the care of the local authority for the purposes of section 15 of the 1968 Act. One consequence of this is that the authority can pass a parental rights resolution in respect of the child, provided, of course, the conditions for this (discussed above) are met.

(8) Duration and review of supervision requirements

The supervision requirement should continue only as long as necessary in the interests of the child. It will lapse automatically after a year unless reviewed and continued within that period, and the reporter has a duty to ensure that each case is reviewed by a hearing at least once a year. The supervision requirement will terminate automatically on the child's 18th birthday. Within the three months before that date the local authority must refer the child to the reporter so that a hearing may be held to advise whether the child needs further supervision or guidance. If the hearing decides that the child does need such guidance or supervision the local authority must provide whatever supervision or guidance the child is prepared to accept.

A residential supervision requirement with a requirement to reside in secure accommodation will lapse unless reviewed and continued within three months, thereafter it must be reviewed every three months.

Review of a supervision requirement may arise in three ways. Firstly, if the local authority considers that the requirement should be reviewed or discharged they must refer the case to the reporter, who will arrange a review hearing. Clearly this means that local authorities should carry out regular reviews of the child's case to ensure that the supervision requirement does not last longer than necessary. Secondly, the child or his/her parents can require that a review is held three months from the date of the requirement being imposed, three months after a review hearing which varied the requirement, and six months after a review which simply continued the requirement. Finally, as noted above, if the requirement has not been reviewed in the previous nine months the reporter must arrange for a review before the expiry of 12 months from the date when a hearing last considered the case.

(9) Rights of appeal

Both parents and child have a right of appeal to the sheriff court against any decision of the hearing. This right must be exercised within three weeks of the decision being made. Legal aid will be available for the appeal where the appellant qualifies, and a safeguarder may be appointed if this is necessary. At the appeal the reporter and anyone who has prepared a report for the hearing may be examined by the sheriff. The sheriff may dismiss the appeal or, if not satisfied that the decision of the hearing was justified, may refer the matter back to the hearing for reconsideration or discharge.

Pending the outcome of the appeal an application may be made to the hearing for suspension of the supervision requirement.

Appeals against warrants issued by the children's hearing must be disposed of within three days.

(10) Referrals from the court system

A child under the age of 16 not subject to a supervision requirement who pleads or is found guilty in a criminal court may be referred to a hearing for advice or for disposal. After considering the advice of the hearing the court may refer the case to them for disposal.

Where a child under 16 who is subject to a supervision requirement pleads or is found guilty the High Court may, and sheriff courts must[1], ask the reporter to arrange a hearing to consider the case and give advice on the treatment of the child. On receipt of the advice the case can be referred back to the hearing for disposal.

Summary courts can also refer cases of people between sixteen and seventeen and a half to a hearing for advice if they plead or are found guilty. After receiving the advice the case can be referred to a hearing for disposal.

None of these provisions apply in cases where there is a fixed penalty, eg murder or certain minor traffic offences.

5. COURT ORDERS PLACING CHILDREN IN CARE

(1) Under the Criminal Procedure (Scotland) Act 1975

Children remanded in custody by criminal courts are to be remanded to the care of a local authority. If the child is between 14 and 16 and the court certifies that the child is unruly or depraved he or she may be held in a remand centre if the court has been notified of the availability of a place there[2].

Where a child is convicted in a summary court he/she may be

1 The district court cannot deal with cases involving children under 16; see ch 1, pt 7(1).
2 Criminal Procedure (Scotland) Act 1975, ss24, 297.

sentenced to up to one years detention with the place and conditions of detention to be decided by the local authority.[1]

A child who has been arrested and not liberated is to be detained in a place of safety unless the child is so unruly that he/she cannot be so detained, it is impractical to detain him/her in a place of safety, or it is inadvisable to detain them in a place of safety because of his/her health or mental or bodily condition[2]. In common with others detained he/she must be brought to court on the next lawful day.

Social work involvement includes the negotiation for the most appropriate resource for the child. Detention of a child through court proceedings may be experienced as especially traumatic by the child and family and so there may be a need for a social worker to become further involved with them, for example in supporting them through the court process, in clarifying the meaning and implications of any order made, and in making practical arrangements as for visits.

(2) Following custody applications[3]

In cases involving applications for custody of children, whether as actions in their own right or ancillary to other actions (eg divorce) the court may make an order committing the child to the care of the local authority rather than granting custody to either of the parties to the case. Such an order may be made in exceptional circumstances where it is impractical or undesirable for the child to be entrusted to either of the parties. There is also provision, where custody is granted to one of the parties, for the child to be placed under the supervision of the local authority. Orders of either type are very rare[4].

6. CHILDREN IN CARE

(1) The welfare principle

In relation to **all** children in care it is important that the requirements of section 20 of the 1968 Act are borne in mind. This section requires the local authority, in taking any decision about a child in care, to give first consideration to the need to safeguard and promote the welfare of

1 Ibid, s413, as amended by the Criminal Justice (Scotland) Act 1987.
2 Criminal Procedure (Scotland) Act 1975, s296.
3 See also ch 3, pt 1(6).
4 Matrimonial Proceedings (Children) Act 1958, ss10, 12; Guardianship Act 1973, s11.

the child throughout his/her childhood. The authority must also, as far as practicable, ascertain the wishes and feelings of the child regarding the decision and give these wishes and feelings due consideration having regard to the age and understanding of the child.

It is also the duty of the local authority to provide accommodation and maintenance for children in their care (including those who are subject to supervision requirements) which in practice means that financial assistance may be given to children in care when required[1].

(2) Placing children in care in residential establishments

Aside from any departmental procedures, the Social Work (Residential Establishments – Child Care) (Scotland) Regulations 1987[2] impose certain requirements which must be fulfilled before a child can be placed in a residential establishment. The regulations apply to children in care under sections 15 and 16, those in care under a place of safety order, those in care as a result of the provisions considered in part 5(2) above, and children for whom the local authority is responsible as a result of respite care arrangements made at the request of their parents. The placing of children in residential establishments by a hearing has been considered above[3].

The precise requirements depend on whether the child has been in care more than six weeks prior to the placement and if so, the following are the requirements:

(a) To ascertain, as far as reasonably practical, the information set out in Schedule 2 to the Regulations. This includes information about the child and his/her family, the child's wishes in respect of residential care and a comprehensive medical report.
(b) To be satisfied that a residential placement is appropriate to the child's needs, taking into account all relevant information and the provisions of section 20 of the 1968 Act.
(c) To be satisfied that the particular placement is appropriate to the child's needs.

Where the child has been in care less than six weeks the authority must simply be satisfied that the placement would not be detrimental to the welfare of the child and that, in light of the available information, the placement would be in the child's best interests. The full procedure must, however, be carried out before the child has been in

1 1968 Act, s21.
2 SI 1987/2233.
3 See pt 4(7).

care for more than six weeks, unless the child is in care following a place of safety order or a warrant from a children's hearing.

There are also two general requirements to be taken account of before making a placement. The first of these is the child's religion, and the second is that children from the same family should generally be kept together.

Once the placement has been made the following must be notified:

(a) The local authority if it is not the care authority.
(b) The education authority if the child is of school age.
(c) The local health authority.
(d) The child's parents or guardian unless this would not be in the best interests of the child.

Where the placement is intended to be for less than 28 days the notifications required by (b) and (c) need not generally be made.

The placement must be monitored to ensure that it continues to be in the child's best interests and in particular:

(a) The child must be visited within one week of the placement being made and then every 3 months, and on such other occasions as the authority considers necessary.
(b) A written report must be produced on each of these visits.

If it ceases to be in the best interests of the child the placement must be terminated as soon as practicable and notification of termination sent to all those originally notified of the placement.

The person in charge of the residential establishment must be given full information about the child when the placement is made and must also agree arrangements for any parental access, the child's education, and medical and dental treatment.

(3) Review of children in care

The cases of children in care under sections 15 and 16 must be reviewed by the authority every six months. Guidelines for the conduct of reviews were issued in May 1984. It should be noted, however, that this **statutory** requirement does not extend to children in care under a supervision requirement. However, in a circular in 1984 it was stated that '[The Secretary of State] hopes ... that local authorities will continue to make progress, as resources permit, towards reviewing the cases of children subject to supervision requirements at intervals of no more than six months.' Where a child is already in care under section 15 when the supervision order is imposed, the statutory six monthly review requirement **will** apply. Most authorities have established and developed procedures and guidelines to facilitate this review process.

(4) Use of secure accommodation[1]

As we have already seen, placement in secure accommodation can be a condition of a residential supervision requirement. Children in care of the local authority under other provisions, eg a residential supervision requirement without such a condition, sections 15, 16 and 44(1)(a) of the 1968 Act, can also be placed in secure accommodation.

Before children in these categories can be placed in secure accommodation both the director of social work and the person in charge of the residential establishment providing the secure accommodation must be satisfied that the placement is in the child's best interests and that either:

(a) the child has a history of absconding, is likely to abscond unless kept in secure accommodation, and if he/she absconds it is likely that his/her welfare will be at risk; or
(b) the child is likely to injure him/herself or others unless he/she is kept in secure accommodation[2].

Before any child is placed in secure accommodation a full assessment of his/her needs must be made and any placement will normally include screening procedures within the social work department (eg the secure accommodation screening group in Strathclyde which may include a senior psychologist, someone from the regional child care team and the head of the establishment).

Once a child has been placed in secure accommodation he/she must be given an explanation in terms he/she can understand and immediate notification must be made to the child's parents and the reporter. A full report must be made to the reporter within 48 hours.

If the child put in secure accommodation is already subject to a supervision requirement the child can only be kept there for seven days unless a continuation is ordered by a hearing. The seven day period is reduced by any period spent in secure accommodation within the preceding 28 days.

1 1968 Act, ss58A–G, inserted by the Health and Social Services and Social Security Adjudication Act 1983, s3. See also pts 4(7) and (8) above.
2 Secure Accommodation (Scotland) Regulations 1983, SI 1983/1912, regs 6, 7, 9; as amended by Secure Accommodation (Scotland) Regulations 1988, SI 1988/841; see also the 1968 Act, s58A(3).

In other cases the reporter must decide what to do within 72 hours of detention, and if the case is to go to a hearing the hearing must take place within seven days. If the reporter decides to take no action the child must be released immediately.

In both cases the parents have a right to require an earlier hearing which must be held on the first lawful day after the request is made.

The children's hearing and sheriff on issuing warrants for the detention or continued detention of a child taken into care on a place of safety order or warrant[1], following a hearing to establish the grounds of referral[2], or pending the disposal of a case by the hearing[3] may order that the child is placed in secure accommodation[4]. Before making such an order the sheriff/hearing must be satisfied as regards the criteria explained above.

A child detained on a place of safety order[5] and whose case has not yet gone before a children's hearing may also be placed in secure accommodation. This can only be done if the director of social work and the manager of the establishment providing the secure accommodation are satisfied that this is in the child's best interests and that the criteria above have been fulfilled. Where such a child is placed in secure accommodation the parents must be informed forthwith and the reporter must, if he/she considers that the child may be in need of compulsory measures of care, arrange a hearing for the first lawful day after the child's detention starts. In cases where the holding of a hearing on the first lawful day would not be in the child's interests the hearing may take place on the following day[6]. If the reporter decides to take no further action, then, as in all place of safety cases, the child must be released.

In all cases the child is to be kept in secure accommodation only at such times as the person in charge of the establishment where he or she is staying, with the agreement of the director of social work, considers necessary.

Children sentenced by the courts[7] may also be kept in secure accommodation.

1 See pt 3.
2 See pt 4(6).
3 See pt 4(5).
4 1968 Act, s58E.
5 1968 Act, s37.
6 Secure Accommodation (Scotland) Regulations 1983, SI 1983/1912, reg 14.
7 See ch 6, pt 7(3).

(5) Parental rights and children in care

The law in this area is far from clear, except in the area of assumption of parental rights where it is clear that the care authority enjoys almost the full range of parental rights and that the parent's rights are restricted to those specifically mentioned in the 1968 Act.

As far as other children in care are concerned the law appears to be that parent(s) retain the full complement of parental rights, but that their ability to exercise some of them may be suspended. For example custody and access may be affected by a place of safety order or the terms of a residential supervision requirement.

On the other hand, the position of the care authority is not clearly stated. Their duties in relation to children in care are spelled out in a number of places, for example section 20A of the 1968 Act and the Boarding-Out and Fostering of Children (Scotland) Regulations 1985[1]. Their rights and powers are not so clearly explained, particularly as they interact with those of the parent(s) of the child. By implication they have the rights necessary for them to carry out their duties to the child, but the precise scope of these are unclear. One example of an area where there is doubt about the powers of local authorities is consent to non-emergency medical treatment/examination. In the case of emergencies no difficulty arises as there is a right to give emergency treatment without consent, as also exists in relation to adults. But for children in care under a place of safety order or under section 15 of the 1968 Act the local authority has no apparent authority to consent to non-emergency medical treatment or examination, though, of course, the child may be mature enough to consent on his/her own behalf. For children under supervision it has been suggested that local authorities have a duty to ensure that the child gets any necessary medical care and treatment[2]. Of course, non-essential treatment could, arguably, be justified by the authority's duty under section 20, and it is certainly suggested in the fostering regulations that the authorities have certain duties in relation to routine medical and dental treatment. The *Review of Child Care Law in Scotland*, issued by the Scottish Office, has, however, indicated the necessity and desirability of clarifying the powers of local authorities by legislation which would, for example, specifically permit medical examination on reception into care under a place of safety order. In practice, difficulties over consent to the treatment of children in care

1 See below pt 7(2).
2 *Strathclyde Regional Council v R*, quoted in B Kearney *Children's Hearings and the Sheriff Court* (1987) p 136.

may not arise because of the widespread practice of getting a parent to sign a blanket consent to medical treatment on reception of the child into care. Since, as we have seen, parents (in the legal sense discussed above) can exercise their rights independently, the consent of only one of the child's parents is needed. In any event, good practice suggests that whenever possible, parents of children in care should be party to decisions about medical treatment.

(6) Aftercare

The local authority is also enabled to provide support, advice and guidance to young people under 21 who have been in their care.[1] In practice, this often means that counselling and financial help is provided to children leaving the care of the local authority and sometimes to children who had been in care some years previously.

7. FOSTERING

(1) Introduction

Fostering describes the situation where a child is placed in the care of someone other than his/her parent(s). The foster parent(s) have the responsibility for caring for the child, but they do not automatically acquire any parental rights, for example to custody of the child. Fostering is therefore different from adoption where, as we have seen[2], the adoptive parent(s) effectively replace the child's natural parent(s) in the eyes of the law. During the period of fostering, particularly where the child is in care, arrangements will usually be made to ensure regular contact between the child and his/her parent(s).

There are two legal provisions governing fostering. The Boarding-Out and Fostering of Children (Scotland) Regulations 1985[3] covers fostering of children in care, and the Fostering (Scotland) Act 1984 and regulations made under it govern private fostering.

1 Section 24 of the 1968 Act.
2 See ch 3, pt 3.
3 SI 1985/1799.

(2) Placements covered by the Boarding-Out and Fostering of Children (Scotland) Regulations 1985

As we have noted these regulations cover fostering of children in care. More specifically they regulate the fostering of children in local authority care, in the care of voluntary organisations, and children subject to a supervision requirement with a condition requiring residence in a foster home.

The regulations deal with three main areas: the approval of foster parents; the making of placements and the provision of information to children's hearings to enable them to make a placement; and the supervision and termination of a placement.

(a) Approval of foster parents

Certain procedures must be followed before approved foster parents are selected. Approval will only be given after a thorough investigation by the care authority (ie the local authority or voluntary organisation) and after consideration of the prospective foster parents by the care authority's fostering panel. These investigations are normally undertaken by experienced social workers, may continue over a period of months, and are informed by guidelines from British Agencies for Adoption and Fostering. The fostering panel is a panel set up to advise on the suitability of prospective foster parents. Although this is the only function mentioned in the regulations they may also be asked to give advice on other matters related to fostering. These panels are normally composed of specialist advisors, social work department line managers, representatives from other professions like medicine and child guidance, and local councillors.

As we will see not all fostering placements will or need be with approved foster parents, but only approved foster parents can be paid a fostering allowance.

Foster parents may be approved for all types of fostering or for specific types of fostering, eg emergency fostering, or even for a specific child.

(b) Making placements: placement by care authority

The precise procedures to be followed depend on the length of time the child has been in the care of the care authority. Where the child has been in care for more than six weeks he or she must be placed with an approved foster parent. Where the child has been in care less than six weeks the foster parent(s) need not be approved before the child is placed, but if the child is to remain in the placement for longer than six weeks the foster parent(s) must go through the full approval procedure. The rationale behind this provision is that it may be desirable for a child who has only recently come into care to be placed with a relative who will not necessarily be an approved foster parent.

In both cases before making the placement the care authority must be satisfied that the placement is in the best interests of the child and in cases where the foster parents are not approved they must also interview the prospective foster parents and visit their house. Apart from the suitability of the foster parents and the foster home the authority must take into account the child's religious persuasion and the desirability of keeping siblings together before making a placement.

It is also possible, where this is thought to be in the child's best interests, to make an emergency placement without making any checks on the foster parents. Checks must then be made within three days, followed by full approval if the placement is going to last longer than six weeks.

Most authorities have specific procedural guidelines for the placement of children and have developed enormously detailed forms which regularise the collection of information which will be important for foster parents to know about the child and his/her family.

(c) *Making placements: placements by children's hearings*

In this case the actual placement is made by a children's hearing rather than a care authority. The hearing, however, must not make a requirement to reside with foster parents (ie someone other than the child's parent or guardian) without first considering a report and recommendation from the social work department. The report should consider the child's needs and the suitability of the foster parents and foster home to meet those needs. The hearing need not follow a recommendation for a fostering placement.

The placement made by the hearing will not necessarily be with approved foster parents and where the prospective foster parents are not approved they must be interviewed and their home visited in the process of compiling the report. In either case the social worker must be satisfied with the proposed placement and satisfied that it is in the best interests of the child before recommending it.

(d) *Making placements: general*

Before a child is placed with foster parents he/she must be medically examined.

Once a child has been placed with foster parents an agreement must be drawn up between the foster parents and the care authority. This must deal with any financial arrangements, arrangements for contact between the child and his/her parents and the arrangements to be made to ensure that the child receives proper education and medical and dental care. In relation to medical and dental care the Regulations in fact impose a duty on the care authority to ensure that the child receives adequate treatment during the fostering placement. The agreement with the foster parents can also deal with any other matter which is thought to be necessary or appropriate. When it is agreed that fostering allowances are to be paid, these are intended to enable the foster parents to maintain the foster child at a level which is commensurate with the level common to their locality, so that a foster child will not necessarily face further stigmatisation on the grounds of his/her clothes/toys. These payments are normally on a sliding scale dependent upon the child's age. Foster parents rarely if ever find these payments to be excessive and many find that not even their costs are met by the payments.

(e) *Supervision and termination of placements*

Once a placement has been made, whether directly or by a hearing, the child must be visited within the first seven days, and thereafter at least every three months. Visits may have to be made more frequently if this is necessary to supervise the welfare of the child and provide support and assistance to the foster parents. The visiting social worker must prepare a report after each visit and these reports must be monitored by the care authority. The importance of these provisions from a social work point of view is that the fostered child remains in the legal care of the care authority and that they are ultimately responsible for his/her welfare.

Where a placement has been made directly by a care authority the child must be removed from the foster home if the care authority consider that the placement is no longer in the best interests of the child.

Where the child has been placed in accordance with a supervision requirement and the local authority consider the placement no longer to be in the child's best interests they must refer the case to the reporter so that a hearing to review the requirement can be held.

Increasingly there has been an acceptance that foster parents enter a partnership with the social work department in the care of children and that some of the implications of this are that they must be more fully briefed about the background of children and more fully involved in the forward planning for children in their care.

(2) Private fostering

It is possible for fostering to be arranged privately and for situations which are legally defined as private fostering to arise without any necessary intention on the part of those involved.

Private fostering is regulated by the Fostering (Scotland) Act 1984 and the Foster Children (Private Fostering)(Scotland) Regulations 1985[1]. These will apply in general to any situation where a child under the age of 16 is being cared for by someone other than a relative or guardian for more than one month. There are certain exceptions to this covering, for example, children at boarding school, children in hospital and children placed for adoption.

Where it is intended to place a child in private fostering at least two weeks notice must be given to the local authority. The authority then has certain duties, including the following:

(a) To find out as far as possible, bearing in mind the age and understanding of the child, his/her wishes and feelings in relation to the proposed placement.
(b) To interview the proposed foster parents and satisfy themselves as to the suitability of the foster home.
(c) To satisfy themselves that the placement will not be detrimental to the child's welfare.
(d) To decide whether the placement is appropriate to the child's needs.

The decision as to whether the placement is appropriate must be communicated to those involved, and the authority may seek to have changes made to make the placement more appropriate or better able to promote the welfare of the child. If necessary the authority can prohibit the placement if they consider that it would be detrimental to the child.

Certain types of person cannot act as foster parents. These include: people convicted of Schedule 1 offences, anyone who has previously had a foster child removed from his/her care, anyone who has had a child removed from his/her care under a supervision requirement, and anyone in respect of whom a parental rights resolution has been passed.

Once a placement has been made the authority must visit the child within seven days, then every three months for the first year and subsequently every six months. Other visits may be made as the authority think necessary. If, as a result of these visits, the authority

1 SI 1985/1798.

consider that the placement is no longer in the child's interests they must notify the foster parents of this.

The local authority can apply to the sheriff court for an order removing the child to a place of safety if the child is kept, or is about to be kept, by any person who is unfit to have his/her care, by anyone who falls into one of the categories prohibited from being a foster parent, or in any premises or environment likely to be detrimental to the child.

Where the child is in imminent danger a place of safety order may be made by a justice of the peace on the application of anyone entitled to visit the child. Such a person may also apply for a place of safety warrant under the Criminal Procedure (Scotland) Act 1975 if they are not permitted to visit a foster child or inspect premises. Such a refusal to allow a visit or inspection will be grounds for granting such a warrant.

The place of safety order will apply until other arrangements can be made for the child, and any child removed from private fostering may be received into care by the local authority under section 15 of the 1968 Act.

APPENDIX

Offences under Schedule 1 of the Criminal Procedure (Scotland) Act 1975

(a) *Any offence under the Sexual Offences (Scotland) Act 1976 committed against someone under 17*. These offences include:

(1) Procuring for the purposes of prostitution or unlawful intercourse.
(2) Procuring by the use of threats, intimidation or false pretences, or using drugs to facilitate unlawful intercourse.
(3) A group of offences introduced by the Incest and Related Offences (Scotland) Act 1986. These include sexual intercourse within the forbidden degrees of relationship, intercourse with a step-child under the age of 21 or who has lived in the same household as the step-parent while under 18, and intercourse by a person in a position of trust (eg a foster parent) with someone under 16 living in the same household as him or her.
(4) Intercourse with a girl under 13.
(5) Intercourse with a girl between the ages of 13 and 16. The difference between this and (4) above is that certain defences are available in this case.

(6) Indecent behaviour towards a girl between 12 and 16. This is now covered more comprehensively in paragraph (*e*) below.
(7) Abduction of a girl under the age of 18 with the intention of having sexual intercourse.
(8) Unlawful detention in a brothel or for the purposes of having unlawful intercourse.
(9) Permitting a girl under 16 to use premises for the purposes of unlawful sexual intercourse.
(10) Encouraging the seduction or prostitution of, unlawful intercourse with, or indecent assault on, a girl under 16.
(11) Allowing a child between the ages of 4 and 16 to reside in or frequent a brothel.

(*aa*) *Any offence under section 80(7) of the Criminal Justice (Scotland) Act 1980*. These involve the commission or procuring of a homosexual act –

(1) Otherwise than in private.
(2) Without the consent of both parties.
(3) With a person under 21.
(4) Between crew members of any UK ship.

(*c*) *Any offence under ss12, 15, 22 or 33 of the Children and Young Persons (Scotland) Act 1937.*

(1) Section 12 makes it an offence for someone over 16 having custody care or charge of a child to assault, ill-treat, abandon, or expose the child in a manner likely to cause unnecessary suffering or injury to the health (including mental health) of the child. Procuring the commission of any of these acts is also an offence. Aside from any other circumstances where it might be established, neglect is deemed to take place in two cases. Firstly, where the person legally liable to maintain a child has failed to provide or procure the provision of (eg by obtaining available benefits) adequate food, clothing or medical aid for the child. Secondly, where the death of a child is caused by suffocation (other than that involving a foreign body) and the child at the time of death was sharing a bed with someone over the age of 16 who was under the influence of drink when he or she went to bed.
(2) Section 15 makes it an offence to cause or allow a child to beg or be used for begging.
(3) Section 22 deals with the situation where a child under seven is left in a room with an improperly guarded open grate fire without reasonable precautions being taken against the risk of burning or

scalding. An offence is committed if the child is killed or suffers serious injury.

(4) Section 33 makes it an offence to allow a child under 16 to take part in a performance where his or her life or limb is endangered.

(d) *Any offence involving bodily injury to a child under 17.*

(e) *Any offence involving the use of lewd, indecent or libidinous practices or behaviour towards a child under the age of 17 years.*

In addition section 52 of the Civic Government (Scotland) Act 1982 provides that references to Schedule 1 offences in the 1968 Act are to include the offences which it creates in relation to the taking, distribution, possession or publication of indecent photographs of children under the age of 16.

5. Special needs

1. INTRODUCTION

This chapter is concerned with the law relevant to those who have special needs arising from some form of disability, either physical or mental, from mental health problems, and as a result of advancing age. Although the chapter has been divided into a number of headings for ease of presentation, this is an area, particularly in relation to persons who are elderly, where any of the pieces of legislation might provide options for a range of individuals. The statutory provisions should, therefore, be viewed as a whole. It is also recognised that although there are some transferable concepts concerning the value base, the sources of knowledge and the various skills required for social workers working with persons with special needs, there are also some important differences and specific skills and knowledge which are necessary.

Legal terminology in this field differs significantly from social work terminology which reflects the value base and current thinking. While social workers may refer to persons with a mental handicap as persons with a learning difficulty, the obvious point is that it is necessary to know the appropriate legal terminology in order to locate and use the relevant law. Traditionally in Scotland the local authority has been the primary provider of services for persons with special needs, but clearly the future will see the diversification of provision of these services into the voluntary and private sectors with the local authority retaining the role of overseeing and providing packages of care utilising all sources of provision for persons in need.

In this situation, where the social work department may well be the supplier of a service or facility and the promoter of the rights of the user, extra care must be taken to acknowledge and respond to users' needs and wishes.

2. ASSESSMENTS

(1) Assessments under section 12A of the Social Work (Scotland) Act 1968

In terms of the new section 12A added to the Social Work (Scotland) Act 1968 by the NHS and Community Care Act 1990, local authorities will, from 1 April 1993, have a duty to carry out assessments of needs in respect of anyone who appears to be in need of 'community care services'. Indeed, the carrying out of an assessment is made a prerequisite for the provision of such services, except in emergencies, and even then an assessment must be carried out as soon as practicable afterwards. In practice these assessments will be carried out by social workers.

The term 'community care services' covers services, other than services for children, provided under Part II of the 1968 Act or under sections 7, 8 and 11 of the Mental Health (Scotland) Act 1984. The services provided under Part II of the 1968 Act include those provided by virtue of section 12[1]; provision of residential care and domiciliary and laundry services, probation and supervision services, and burial and cremation of people in the care of or receiving assistance from the local authority. The provisions of the 1984 Act cover local authority functions, provision of aftercare services for those suffering from mental disorder and training and occupation for those with a mental handicap[2].

The process of assessment is in two stages. First, the assessment is carried out by the social work department. Second, on the basis of the assessment the authority must decide whether the needs of the person call for the provision of community care services. There is no right to insist on the provision of certain services based on the outcome of the assessment. Provision of services is, to a large extent, at the discretion of the local authority. The remedies available to someone who is disappointed at the outcome of the assessment process are either to seek judicial review of the authority's decision or to make representations under the representations procedure which has operated in all local authorities since 1 April 1991[3]. Evidence from England is beginning to emerge demonstrating the remedy of judicial review. People who have been assessed as in need of services and have not then been pro-

1 See ch 1, pt 15.
2 See below, pt 6.
3 See ch 1, pt 15.

vided with those services are pursuing civil law suits against the relevant authority[1].

The statutory provision also lays down some requirements for the conduct of the assessment process. No decision that a person requires nursing care can be made without consulting a medical practitioner. Where it appears that any person being assessed may be in need of services provided by the health board or a housing authority, the social work department must discover from them what services are likely to be made available to the person being assessed and that information will be taken into account in making the assessment. Finally, if the person being assessed has a mental and/or physical impairment, the provisions of the Disabled Persons (Services, Consultation and Representation) Act 1986 will apply to the assessment (see below).

The local authority has been named the lead agency with the remit to organise and co-ordinate the provision of packages of care for persons in need. This highlights further the difficulties inherent in the situation when the local authority has a duty to provide various services and is also the body responsible for upholding the rights of users. Conflict of interest and the difficulties of enforcing such statutes additionally complicates this situation.[2]

It is then envisioned that the social worker as case manager will use the full systemic assessment of client needs to plan and co-ordinate the delivery of the matching resources provided by the social work department, voluntary bodies and/or private agencies. There is the hope that unmet needs can be more readily identified and will influence the purchasing strategies. Case managers are also expected to monitor the quality of care provided and to review the needs of the client.

(2) Disabled Persons (Services, Consultation and Representation) Act 1986

This allows a person who has a mental and/or physical impairment or someone who cares for him/her to request an assessment by the local authority of the need for services provided under section 2 of the Chronically Sick and Disabled Persons Act 1970 (see below). The assessment must take into account the ability of the present carer to

1 See for example *Community Care* 4/6/92.

2 See discussion in *Contracting and Case Management in Community Care – The Challenges for Local Authorities* by Edward Peck, Pete Ritchie and Helen Smith – CCETSW Paper 32, January 1992.

continue to provide care. The 1986 Act contains detailed provisions allowing challenge of the assessment and the authority's proposals in relation to the provision of services. The government has indicated that this section will not be brought into force, taking the view that the representation process under the 1968 Act is adequate for this purpose. The needs and interests of persons who are disabled were to have become much more recognised through this statute and through the appropriate social work advocacy, but for a number of reasons, including lack of resources and the low priority that work with persons who are disabled has in social work departments, this has not happened to the extent intended. Clearly, however, these provisions should prove to be of increasing relevance to social workers as the proportion of persons with increasingly severe disabling conditions who are discharged from long-stay institutions and into the community is growing and the expectations about the involvement of social workers will also multiply.

3. GENERAL PROVISIONS ON DISABILITY

(1) Chronically Sick and Disabled Persons Act 1970

The introduction of this Act marked a turning point in the provision of services and facilities for persons with special needs with a shift in thinking about persons with sometimes quite overwhelming disabilities being supported and empowered to live as independently as possible in the community. The relatively low uptake of the provisions of the Act will be discussed below.

The legislation imposes a number of duties on social work authorities and others. A large part of it is taken up with the provision of access to buildings for disabled people with the main provisions of relevance here being found in sections 1 and 2.

Section 1 imposes a general duty on local authorities to investigate the need for services to persons with handicapping conditions in their area. This requires that the authority find out the number of such people in the area and assesses the need for services for them. A curiosity of the Act is that there is no definition of handicap or disability.

Section 2 is concerned with social work department duties to provide specific services to individuals. It requires them, where they are satisfied as to need, to arrange for the following: provision of practical assistance in the home; provision of, or assistance in obtaining, wireless, television, library or other recreational facilities; provision of lectures, games or other recreational facilities outwith the disabled person's home; provision of assistance in taking advantage of educational facilities; assistance with travel to make use of services provided by the local authority; assistance in adapting the home or in the provision of additional facilities designed to secure the greater safety, comfort or convenience of a disabled person; assistance in taking holidays; provision of meals; and provision of assistance in obtaining a telephone and any adaptation necessary to allow its use. Many of these **duties** will be very familiar to local authority social workers and occupational therapists.

Section 2 also has relevance in that the assessment carried out under the Disabled Persons (Services, Consultation and Representation) Act 1986 is designed to identify the need for any of these services. One drawback of the provision is the lack of a simple and effective remedy to enforce rights. A disabled person who is denied assistance may make use of the representations procedure or seek judicial review, but even if they do, the authority may still be constrained by lack of resources. Social workers may find themselves as the gatekeepers for tightly rationed resources. A further drawback is the likelihood that these duties will suffer by the place they assume in the hierarchy of social work department priorities and the allocation of work of this nature to unqualified or less experienced staff.

(2) Disabled Persons (Employment) Act 1944

This provides for a quota system for the employment of disabled people, and requires that at least 3% of the workforce employed by employers of more than 20 people consists of people registered as disabled. Two points should be noted. In the first place the legislation refers to those who register with the Employment Service as disabled, rather than all those who are disabled but do not register. Secondly, employers are able to obtain permits exempting them from the quota requirement. The other aspect of the Act is the provision for training of disabled people and provision of employment rehabilitation centres and ASSET centres. Assistance for disabled people should be available through Jobcentres, with a network of disablement resettlement officers available for those with special problems.

Both aspects of the Act have come in for considerable criticism and are generally regarded as having been ineffective in providing employment opportunities for disabled people[1].

1 See, for example, National Audit Office *Department of Employment and Manpower Services Commission: Employment Assistance to Disabled Adults* HC (1986–87) no 367.

Many local authorities provide sheltered employment for people with disabilities.

(3) Services provided under the Social Work (Scotland) Act 1968

Local authorities can make use of the wide powers to promote social welfare conferred on them by section 12 to provide services for persons who are disabled. This includes providing assistance in cash or kind to prevent future greater expense to the department, since the 'persons in need' to whom such aid is available include people 'suffering from a mental disorder or substantially handicapped by any deformity or disability' as well as those in need of care and attention arising out of infirmity[1]. More specifically, local authorities have a duty to provide domiciliary services (formerly home helps) and laundry services to households where these are necessary because a person in need lives there[2].

(4) Special educational needs

The Education (Scotland) Acts 1980 and 1981 require education authorities to make provision for special educational need. The term 'special need' covers children who either have learning difficulties or who suffer from a disability or handicap which prevents them from making use of normal educational provision.

The education authority has a duty to carry out assessments of children aged two or over who come to their attention as having or appearing to have special educational needs. The object of the assessment is to discover if the child has pronounced, specific or complex special educational needs which require continuing review. The assessment involves medical and psychological examination and if, on conclusion of the assessment, the authority consider that the child falls into one of the categories listed, a record of needs will be opened for the child. This record of needs will identify the special needs of the child and specify the provisions which the authority will make for the child. Parents have rights of appeal, for example, against a decision to record a child and against the assessment made of a child.

The parents of children have the right to make a placing request for their child to be enrolled in a school of their choice, including a private

1 Section 94(1).
2 Section 14.

school, anywhere in the United Kingdom. The local authority can refuse the request for a number of defined reasons, eg that the authority can cater adequately for the child's needs at a school of their own.

In the period starting two years and finishing nine months before the 16th birthday of a child with a record of need, a 'future needs assessment' must be carried out for the child. The objective of the future needs assessment is to identify educational and training provision which would benefit the child on leaving school. The assessment involves both the education department and the social work department. As part of the process reference must be made to the latter for an opinion as to whether the child is disabled. If they consider that the child is disabled they must then carry out their own assessment of the child's needs. Typically, a social worker will meet with the parents and the young adult involved shortly before the school leaving date. It is important that the social worker discuss the projected needs of the young adult with all persons concerned and that includes the young adult. It is also crucial for the social worker to recognise that this interview may well be viewed as an intrusion and unwelcome intervention, particularly in situations where the social work department has had little previous contact with the family.

Similar reference to the social work department is necessary where the education authority intend to record a child for the first time within the period noted above. The social work department must be notified six months before any person, on whom they have given an opinion that he/she is disabled, ceases full-time school education.

4. MENTAL ILLNESS AND HANDICAP: COMPULSORY ADMISSION TO HOSPITAL

(1) Introduction

It is vital that all local authority social workers understand the powers which enable them to intervene in the lives of persons who are experiencing mental health problems or persons with learning difficulties. The limits of these powers are equally significant in acknowledging and upholding the civil liberties of clients. This area of work is considered to be especially complex and difficult not least in that social workers become involved in the process of persons losing their liberty. A local authority social worker will undertake further education and training to become a recognised mental health officer before being authorised to use such powers.

Before anyone can be made subject to compulsory admission to hospital or guardianship he/she must be suffering from a mental disorder. 'Mental disorder' is defined as 'any mental illness or handicap however caused or manifested'. With two exceptions, no further legal definition of mental illness or mental handicap is offered. The first exception relates to the definitions of mental handicap amounting to mental impairment and severe mental impairment. Secondly, it is specifically provided that a person is not to be treated as suffering from a mental disorder **by reason only** of promiscuity or other immoral conduct, sexual deviancy, or dependence on drugs or alcohol. There is no lower age limit for compulsory admission to hospital.

Compulsory admission (and some aspects of guardianship, see below) is governed by the Mental Health (Scotland) Act 1984. At this stage it should be noted that well over 90% of those admitted to hospital suffering from mental illness or mental handicap are admitted as voluntary patients. On the other hand, there are also arguments that the local authority has not sufficiently used its powers to intervene to protect some of the most vulnerable and needy people in the community.

(2) Grounds for admission

Compulsory admission to hospital can take one of two forms: admission following application to the sheriff court[1] or emergency admission[2]. However, before either of these can take place certain grounds relating to the patient's mental condition and need for treatment have to be established.

In the case of admission following application to the sheriff the requirements are[3]:

(a) That the person is suffering from a mental disorder of such a nature and degree as to make hospital treatment appropriate; **and**
(b) it is necessary for the health and safety of that person or for the protection of others that such treatment should be given, and it cannot be given without compulsory admission and detention.

There are two qualifications to the first requirement. Where the disorder is persistent and shows itself only in the form of abnormally aggressive or irresponsible behaviour (what is sometimes referred to as psychopathy), the disorder must be susceptible to treatment.

1 Mental Health (Scotland) Act 1984, s18.
2 Ibid, s24.
3 Ibid, s17.

Secondly, where the disorder takes the form of mental handicap, the handicap must amount to a treatable mental impairment or severe mental impairment.

In the case of emergency admission the requirements are[1]:

(a) That because of the patient's mental disorder it is urgently necessary for his/her health or safety or for the protection of others that he/she should be admitted to a hospital; **and**
(b) that to proceed with an application under section 18 would involve unreasonable delay.

(3) Procedure: application to sheriff[2]

Applications to the sheriff must be made either by the patient's nearest relative or by a mental health officer. The nearest relative is essentially the spouse or relative caring for the patient or, if the patient is not being cared for by a relative, is the relative in the highest category on a list starting with children, parents and siblings. A mental health officer (MHO) is a social worker, employed by a regional or islands council, who has experience of dealing with people with mental health problems, and who represents an independent professional perspective and has received appropriate training. The nearest relative has the power to require the local authority to direct a MHO to investigate the case of an individual with a view to taking proceedings for compulsory admission.

The MHO's investigations will include an interview with the patient and in arriving at the decision as to whether or not to apply for compulsory admission he/she must take into account the wishes of the nearest relative. If the MHO is satisfied that the detention of the patient in hospital is the most appropriate way of providing for his/her care and treatment, the MHO may apply for compulsory admission, and must apply in the circumstances noted in the next paragraph. The nearest relative must be notified of the intention to apply and is entitled to object and be heard at the court hearing. If the MHO decides that it would not be appropriate to apply for compulsory admission, the nearest relative must be informed and he/she may then exercise his/her power to make the application for admission. Whatever the recommendation, it is crucial that the MHO has communicated this and the reasons for the recommendation to the patient and

1 Ibid, s24.
2 Ibid, ss19–21.

nearest relative so that the basis for reciprocal and mutually agreed goals may be established as soon as possible. The MHO will also, when appropriate, make enquiries about alternative provision of services outwith the hospital setting.

The applicant for admission must have seen the patient within 14 days of the application. In addition he/she must have obtained two medical recommendations indicating the form of mental disorder suffered by the patient and which of the grounds of admission applies to him/her. One of these medical reports will normally be given by the patient's general practitioner (GP) and the other by a specialist from the intended place of treatment. The later of the reports must be based on an examination of the patient which took place within seven days of the application, and the earlier examination must be no more than five days before the later. Both reports must agree as to one form of mental disorder suffered by the patient. The MHO must apply for compulsory admission if requested to by one of the doctors providing a report, even if he/she considers compulsory admission unnecessary. These reports will normally be obtained by the MHO as part of his/her investigation of the case.

The application is presented to the sheriff court accompanied by the medical reports and a statement as to the MHO's opinion, which will state the reasons for that opinion. In deciding on the application the sheriff may make any enquiries he/she thinks necessary and must hear any objecting nearest relative, the MHO (if he/she opposes the application), and the patient or patient's representative.

The application for admission must be approved or a hearing on it held within five working days of the submission of the application.

Where the patient is admitted to hospital as a result of an application by the nearest relative, the local authority must be notified of the admission within seven days, and the MHO must interview the patient within a further 21 days and produce a report on the patient known as a social circumstances report. A copy of this report is sent to the responsible medical officer (ie the doctor responsible for treating the patient) and to the Mental Welfare Commission[1]. Although the statutory requirement to produce a social circumstances report only arises where the application for admission is made by the nearest relative, the code of practice issued under the 1984 Act suggests that it is good practice to prepare such a report in respect of all patients compulsorily admitted.

1 See below, pt 6(14).

(4) Procedure: emergency admission[1]

Provided that the grounds for emergency admission are established, the recommendation for admission is made by a single medical practitioner who must have seen the patient on the same day as the recommendation is made. Before making the recommendation the doctor must obtain, where practicable, the consent of a relative **or** the MHO. Although the wording of the Act is not entirely clear it appears that the accepted interpretation is that only one of these consents is needed, and admission can proceed in the face of opposition from the other person able to consent. The Mental Welfare Commission must be notified of the patient's admission, as must, if this has not already happened, the nearest relative or a responsible person living with the patient.

(5) Duration of detention: following application to sheriff[2]

If the sheriff grants the application for admission this is warrant for the detention of the patient for six months. This can be renewed for a further period of six months and, thereafter, for periods of one year.

The procedure for renewal of detention is that the responsible medical officer either examines the patient or obtains a report concerning his/her condition, carries out various consultations with others concerned with the patient's treatment, and then assesses the continued need for detention of the patient. For continued detention to be necessary the grounds for admission must still apply to the patient. If continued detention is considered necessary a report is made to the hospital managers and this, without reference to the sheriff, renews the authority for the patient's detention.

In addition, a review of a patient's case must be undertaken between the third and fourth week of detention to determine the need for continued detention.[3]

(6) Duration of detention: emergency admission[4]

An emergency recommendation is only authority for the detention of the patient for up to 72 hours. This period can, however, be extended

1 Mental Health (Scotland) Act 1984, s24.
2 Ibid, s30.
3 Ibid, s22(4).
4 Ibid, s26.

for a further 28 days[1]. Such further detention can only take place where a report has been produced on the patient which indicates the need for continued detention for a limited time. The consent of the nearest relative or MHO must be obtained if practicable.

Unless the MHO has consented to the continued detention, the local authority must be notified. The MHO must then, within 21 days of the continuation of detention, produce a social circumstances report on the patient. Although the statutory requirement only arises where the MHO has not consented, good practice suggests that such a report should be prepared in all cases.

Previously the position was that a patient detained for the further 28 day period under section 26 had to be released on the expiry of that period, even if his/her condition had deteriorated[2]. The Mental Health Detention (Scotland) Act 1991 introduced a new section 26A to the 1984 Act with effect from 9 March 1992. This provides that such patients may now be detained for a period of three days from the lodging of a report with the sheriff clerk. This detention is only available where no application has been made under section 18 or it is not practicable to make such an application within the 28 days, **and** the patient's condition has deteriorated so that he/she needs to be detained in the interests of his/her own safety or that of others. The consent of the nearest relative or MHO must, if practicable, be obtained. There is a right of appeal to the sheriff.

A further new provision is that an application to the sheriff for admission under section 18 of a patient detained under the emergency provisions outlined above is authority for his/her detention for a period of five days after the submission of the application. Courts must now, of course, deal with such applications within five days.

Concerns have been expressed by MHOs about the use of this emergency detention as an administrative expedient rather than as outlined above and that all the inclusions of the phrase 'where practicable' in gaining the consent of the MHO have served, in practice, to marginalise and even exclude the use and contributions of MHOs[3].

(7) Rights of appeal

The patient has the right to appeal against a report authorising continued detention for 28 days following emergency admission and against renewal of the authority for detention where he/she has been

1 Mental Health (Scotland) Act 1984, s26.
2 *B v Forsey* 1988 SLT 572.
3 'In the Margins' by Nick Clayton, *Community Care* 4/6/92.

detained following application to the sheriff. In the latter case there is a right of appeal once during every period of renewed detention. It should be noted that there is **no** right of appeal against a sheriff's decision to admit the patient to hospital or against an emergency recommendation[1]. In such circumstances it would be open to the patient to seek judicial review of the decision or to exercise the right, which he/she has at all times, to make representations to the Mental Welfare Commission, who have the power to order the patient's discharge from hospital.

(8) Consent to treatment

In general, patients detained following application to the sheriff or for the period of 28 days following emergency admission can be treated for their mental disorder without their consent[2]. There are two categories of exception to this:

(a) *Treatments requiring the patient's consent and a second opinion*[3]. The treatments involved here are psychosurgery and the surgical implantation of hormones to reduce the male sex drive. The patient must consent, and if he/she is incapable of informed consent or refuses to consent the treatment cannot be given. Even if the patient consents, a second opinion supporting the treatment must be obtained from a practitioner appointed by the Mental Welfare Commission. Treatment in this category is very rare.

(b) *Treatment requiring the patients consent or a second opinion*[4]. The treatments referred to here are administration of medicine for more than three months and electro-convulsive treatment (ECT). The patient must either consent or, if the patient refuses or is incapable of giving consent, the treatment must be supported by a second opinion.

Certain urgent treatment, eg to prevent violent behaviour or to prevent deterioration in the patient's condition, may be given without consent, even if it falls into one of these categories. If such treatment is given it must generally be non-hazardous and reversible.

It should be noted that, even though a patient is compulsorily detained, his/her consent must be obtained for any treatment which is not treatment for his/her mental disorder.

1 See *F v Management Committee and Managers, Ravenscraig Hospital* 1989 SLT 49.
2 Mental Health (Scotland) Act 1984, s103.
3 Ibid, s97.
4 Ibid, s98.

(9) Detention by nursing staff[1]

Voluntary patients can be detained by a hospital nurse for up to two hours to prevent them from leaving hospital. This can only be done when it is necessary in the patient's interests or for the protection of others and where the immediate attendance of a doctor (who could recommend emergency admission) cannot be obtained.

(10) Discharge of patients

Discharge of patients can be ordered:

(a) By a sheriff on appeal;
(b) by the responsible medical officer or the Mental Welfare Commission if satisfied **either** that the patient is not suffering from a mental disorder of a type which requires him/her to be liable to be detained in hospital for medical treatment **or** that it is not necessary for the health or safety of the patient or the protection of others that he/she should receive such treatment;
(c) by the nearest relative. The procedure for this is that the nearest relative gives at least seven days notice to the hospital managers. The responsible medical officer can object if satisfied that the grounds of admission still exist, and his/her objection will prevent discharge. The nearest relative can appeal to the sheriff against the prevention of discharge.

(11) Detention by a police constable

Police constables have the power to remove to a place of safety anyone found in a public place who appears to be suffering from mental disorder and to be in immediate need of care and control. Once taken to a place of safety he/she can be detained there for up to 72 hours. In this context a place of safety is a hospital or residential home for those suffering mental disorder, or another suitable place. Those detained are not to be kept in a police station unless in an emergency where there is no other suitable place available. The nearest relative of anyone detained must be informed as soon as possible.

1 Mental Health (Scotland) Act 1984, s25.

(12) Place of safety orders

MHOs have the power to enter any premises where a person suffering from a mental disorder is living if the MHO believes that he/she has been ill-treated or neglected, is not being kept under proper control, or is living alone and uncared for and is unable to care for him/herself. If entry is refused a warrant can be obtained authorising a police officer to enter the house with a doctor. Following such entry the mentally disordered person may be removed to a place of safety and kept there for up to 72 hours.

5. MENTAL ILLNESS AND HANDICAP: GUARDIANSHIP

As an alternative to admission to hospital, people over the age of 16 can be received into guardianship under the Mental Health (Scotland) Act 1984. This is sometimes referred to as mental health guardianship.

(1) Grounds[1]

The grounds for application are that the patient is suffering from a mental disorder of a nature or degree warranting reception into guardianship **and** that it is in the interests of the patient's welfare that he/she should be so received. The first ground will be certified by two medical practitioners, the second is the province of the MHO.

(2) Procedure[2]

The procedure is similar to that involved in compulsory admission and the application can be made either by the MHO or by the nearest relative. An additional duty is imposed on local authorities to satisfy themselves as to the suitability of the proposed guardian. In practice nearly all guardians are regional councils, their social work departments or directors of social work.

Once the application is approved it must be forwarded to the local authority. The powers of the guardian are then to specify the place of

1 Mental Health (Scotland) Act 1984, s36.
2 Ibid, ss37–40.

residence of the patient and to require the patient to attend for education and medical treatment. These powers are limited and exclude, for example, the ability to consent, on the patient's behalf, to beneficial medical treatment. Where it is necessary to seek greater authority to provide day to day help, guidance and supervision, it is possible to apply to the Court of Session for the appointment of a tutor-dative[1].

Patients subject to guardianship are to be supervised by the local authority and this requires at least one visit every three months. The authority can also issue directions to guardians (in the odd case where they are not the guardian) and require them to supply information and reports on the patient.

(3) Duration and appeal[2]

Initially guardianship lasts for six months, but it can be renewed for further periods, initially of six months, and then of one year. The procedure for renewal requires that the patient is examined by the responsible medical officer who reports on his/her condition. If the responsible medical officer is satisfied that the first of the grounds noted above still applies to the patient, he/she will forward the report to the MHO. The MHO will consider whether the second ground still applies, and if it does will report to that effect to the local authority. The report renews authority for guardianship.

There is a right of appeal against renewal of authority for guardianship.

(4) Discharge[3]

Discharge can be ordered by:

(a) The responsible medical officer or the Mental Welfare Commission, if satisfied that the first ground no longer exists;
(b) by the local authority or the Mental Welfare Commission, if satisfied that the second ground no longer exists;
(c) by the sheriff on appeal if satisfied that either or both grounds no longer exist;
(d) by the nearest relative. Fourteen days notice must be given and if the responsible medical officer and the MHO agree that the

1 See below, pt 6(5).
2 Mental Health (Scotland) Act 1984, s47.
3 Ibid, ss50, 51.

grounds for guardianship still exist they can refuse discharge. The nearest relative can appeal to the sheriff.

6. MENTAL DISABILITY

(1) Definitions

In their recent discussion paper on *Mentally Disabled Adults: Legal Arrangements for Managing their Welfare and Finances*[1] the Scottish Law Commission offer the following definitions of legal incapacity and legal disability:

'A person who is mentally incapable or lacks mental capacity is incapable in the legal sense of entering into a transaction or making a decision. This is because the person, due to his or her mental state, cannot understand the nature of the transaction or decision or comprehend its consequences or effects. Transactions or decisions by a mentally incapacitated person are legally ineffective. Few people with a mental illness or mental handicap are so incapacitated that they are unable to make even the simplest decision. The majority have the ability to make some decisions and may be said to be disabled. We use the term "mentally disabled" as a convenient way of referring to those individuals who suffer from total or partial mental incapacity.'[2]

Following on from this there are three important points to note. Firstly that, as far as the law is concerned, mental disability has to do with the ability to understand the meaning and consequences of decisions, whether these are to do with personal matters, such as medical treatment, or financial matters, such as renting accommodation. Secondly, the degree to which mental disability affects individuals varies markedly. Some are only incapable of dealing with decisions which are relatively complex, others are incapable of making, or communicating, **any** decision, however minor. Finally, the way in which the law is used to intervene in the lives of mentally disabled people must be sensitive to these differences in competence and must allow them the greatest say possible in how they live their lives.

(2) The relevant law

This section will concentrate on three areas; personal guardianship, management of affairs and consent to medical treatment. There are,

1 Discussion Paper No 94 (1991).
2 Para 1.2.

however, a number of other statutory provisions which are relevant in this context. These include the Disabled Persons (Services, Consultation and Representation) Act 1986 with its provision for assessments; the Education (Scotland) Act 1980 with its provisions for special educational need, the Chronically Sick and Disabled Persons Act 1970; the provisions of the Mental Health (Scotland) Act 1984 regarding compulsory admission; the provisions for assessment introduced by the NHS and Community Care Act 1990; and the general provisions of the Social Work (Scotland) Act 1968 under which a person suffering mental disorder (which includes mental handicap) is defined as a 'person in need'.

(3) Personal guardianship

Personal guardianship is concerned with decisions affecting the personal life of an individual. This would include decisions about residence, education, employment, medical treatment and with whom that person may associate. As we have already seen parents have, subject to some exceptions, certain rights in respect of these types of decisions as they affect children[1]. Therefore the parents of a mentally disabled person will be able to exercise these powers in respect of their child, probably to a greater extent than if the child was not handicapped. The problem arises in relation to people who are no longer children; no-one has the automatic right to take decisions on behalf of another person. There are, however, people affected by mental disability who will require supervision, guidance and, in some cases, control in the areas mentioned above, and in respect of whom a personal guardian may need to be appointed to do this.

At the moment there are two main types of personal guardians: mental health guardians and tutors-dative. There has been some criticism of the adequacy of the law in this area, and the Scottish Law Commission are currently conducting a public consultation exercise on proposed reforms[2].

(4) Mental health guardians

As is noted above this type of guardian can be appointed where the patient suffers from a mental disorder justifying reception into guardianship

1 See ch3, pt 1(3).
2 See the discussion paper referred to above and A Ward *The Power to Act* (1990) chs 4–6.

and it is in the patient's interest that this should happen. The whole process is overseen by the social work department, and in most cases they will be the guardian appointed. The powers of guardians are limited to deciding where the patient should live, making the patient attend for medical treatment, work, education or training, and ensuring that doctors and the MHO have access to the patient. Guardians therefore do not have a right of custody, ie the power to ensure that the patient stays in a particular place (though they can have the patient brought back if he/she goes away), nor can they consent to beneficial medical treatment on behalf of the patient.

(5) Tutors-dative

A tutor-dative is someone appointed by the Court of Session to act on behalf of a mentally handicapped person. This procedure was revived in 1986 as a way of providing some supervision to mentally handicapped adults, and several appointments have been made since then. In strict law the tutor is appointed for an indefinite period and has the power to act on behalf of the disabled person in all areas of his/her life. In practice the recent appointments have been of tutors with specific powers, which have been detailed in the application for appointment and tailored to the needs of the disabled person, and have generally been for fixed periods.

(6) Management of affairs

The next six sections are concerned with the management of the property and financial affairs of someone suffering from mental disability. The extent to which intervention in one of the forms noted below is necessary will depend on the amount and nature of the individual's property and on the degree of their disability. It will also depend on whether it is possible to manage these affairs through an essentially informal arrangement such as a joint bank account or an account held by someone 'in trust for' the disabled person.

At this stage it is also worth noting that contracts entered into by people suffering from mental disorder may be void. This will be the case if the person was unable to understand the nature of the contract or its effects. Clearly this will depend on the nature of the contract and the degree of disability of the individual concerned. The person wishing to challenge a contract entered into by someone with mental disability has the burden of proving that he/she was incapable of understanding the contract, and until that is done the contract is presumed to be valid.

(7) *Curator bonis*

A *curator bonis* can be appointed to manage the affairs of a person who is incapable of coping with this him/herself. The application for appointment can be made at the sheriff court and must be supported by two medical certificates. Local authorities may come under an obligation to apply for the appointment of a *curator bonis* in respect of an individual where this appears to be necessary and no application has been made by anyone else.

This means of managing the affairs of persons who are disabled has been criticised. It is expensive, and is only really worthwhile if the estate involved exceeds £50,000. The curator may have no expertise in the field of mental disability, and there have been complaints in the past that curators have not met their wards or their families, and have not been responsive to their needs or wishes. A more fundamental difficulty is that appointment of a curator transfers all powers of management to him/her. It therefore does not recognise the possibility that the disabled person may be able to take some decisions independently. Some of these problems can be overcome by sensitivity on the part of the curator, but proposals for reform in this area have been put forward by the Scottish Law Commission.

(8) Management by hospital authorities

Under section 94 of the Mental Health (Scotland) Act 1984 hospital managers have the power to deal with property belonging to patients who are incapable of managing it themselves because of mental disorder. This incapacity is established by a certificate to that effect granted by the doctor in charge of the patient's treatment. These management powers apply automatically to property up to £3,000, but this limit can be increased in individual cases by the Mental Welfare Commission.

(9) DSS appointees

Anyone over the age of 18 may be appointed to deal with Social Security benefits on behalf of someone who is unable to manage his/her own affairs. The appointee is able to apply for, receive and deal with benefits on behalf of the disabled person. The procedure for appointment is simply that the application is made to the DSS on the appropriate form. The Scottish Law Commission notes that this procedure is widely used and that '[a]ppointees are generally relatives, home helps, or managers of residential or nursing homes in which the recipient lives.'[1]

(10) Trusts

Trusts are legal entities which hold and administer property on behalf of someone else, with the administration being carried out by trustees appointed for that purpose. This type of arrangement is favoured by some organisations, such as the Scottish Society for the Mentally Handicapped, as the best way of managing property which a disabled person cannot manage him/herself. The terms of the trust can be designed to meet the specific needs of the individual concerned, and the trustees are not subject to the same detailed rules and supervision as curators. Setting up of a trust requires forward planning, as once property actually belongs to a disabled person who is unable to manage his/her affairs it cannot be transferred to a trust. The reason for this is that the only person who can transfer property to a trust is the owner of the property and the disabled person is unlikely to have the legal capacity to do this. If he/she did have this capacity the trust would probably be unnecessary.

(11) *Negotiorum gestio*

This is a legal principle which allows someone to act on your behalf when you are incapable of acting for yourself, and where, were you able to, you would have authorised them to act on your behalf. The relevance here is that the inability may be due to mental disability and this principle may, for example, allow a friend or relative to act on behalf of someone who is unable to do so themselves.

(12) Power of attorney

This is a written authorisation allowing someone to act and take decisions on your behalf. In order to grant the authorisation you must be legally capable of doing so. A power of attorney could therefore not be granted by someone suffering a disability which deprived him/her of such capacity. On the other hand, once granted, the power of attorney does not terminate if the granter becomes legally incapable of acting. This might therefore be used when someone was aware that at

1 *Mentally Disabled Adults* para 4.15.

some time in the future a disability would deprive him/her of the ability to manage his/her own affairs.

(13) Consent to medical treatment

In general terms medical treatment can only be given with the consent of the patient; further, the consent must be based on an understanding of the treatment and its risks. There are, of course, cases where consent is not necessary; the main examples being emergency treatment and treatment of patients compulsorily detained under the Mental Health (Scotland) Act 1984.

Difficulties can arise in the case of adults with mental disabilities who are unable to give the sort of consent mentioned above. Clearly the extent to which a disability affects the ability to give consent will depend on the nature and extent of the disability and the type of treatment, but obviously problems can arise. When they do there is no one who can consent on behalf of the disabled person, unless a tutor-dative with that specific power has been appointed. In these circumstances the law appears to be that treatment can be given without consent where the treatment is in the patient's best interests in that it is carried out '... in order either to save their lives or to ensure improvement or prevent deterioration in their physical or mental health.'[1]. Ward expresses the view that the English decision which is the basis for this statement would not be followed in Scotland and that a tutor should be appointed to give consent or application made to court for consent in all cases other than emergencies[2].

(14) The Mental Welfare Commission

The Mental Welfare Commission is appointed by the Crown on the recommendation of the Secretary of State. There must be at least three women, three medical practitioners and a solicitor or advocate amongst its members.

The general role of the Mental Welfare Commission is to exercise a protective function in respect of those suffering from mental disorder, and it therefore has an interest in mentally disordered patients whether detained or voluntary patients and whether in hospital or in the community. It is empowered to look into cases of ill-treatment,

1 *F v West Berkshire Health Authority* [1989] 2 All ER 545 at 551c per Lord Brandon.
2 A Ward *The Power to Act* ch 8.

deficiency of care, improper detention and loss of, or damage to, patients property.

The Mental Welfare Commission is also required to: discharge patients if it thinks fit; advise the Secretary of State on the discharge of Secretary of State's patients; visit detained patients and those subject to guardianship orders; adjudicate on the withholding of mail; and consent to treatment where this is necessary as noted in part 4 above.

7. MENTAL ILLNESS AND DISABILITY: OTHER LOCAL AUTHORITY FUNCTIONS AND DUTIES

The provisions which have already been noted in parts 2 and 3 are clearly relevant here. As well as these the social work department has a number of specific responsibilities to those suffering or recovered from mental disorder. These include:

(a) Provision of after care services for persons who are or have been suffering from mental disorder.
(b) To act as parents as regards, for example, visits to any child who is the subject of a parental rights resolution, or to anyone for whom they are a guardian under the Act, who is admitted to hospital.
(c) Provision of suitable training and occupation for people over the age of 16 who suffer from mental handicap(learning difficulties).

Increasingly these provisions are becoming more central as the emphasis shifts away from institutional care for persons with mental health problems and persons with learning difficulties. Local authority social workers who are not MHOs are encountering more and more situations in which such persons are finding themselves to be homeless, misplaced in the prisons and within the community with few appropriate resources.

8. OLD AGE

(1) Introduction

Persons who are elderly are a large and growing group within society. Currently about 15% of the population is over the age of 65, and the number involved will grow significantly by the beginning of the next century. There is very little specific legal provision for elderly persons in contrast, for example, to the volume of law relating to children.

Attention is drawn to all of the preceding sections in this chapter which refer to provisions which may be relevant to a person suffering disability because of his/her age. It should also be remembered that the definition of 'person in need' in the 1968 Act refers specifically to those 'in need of care and attention arising out of ... age'. This provision must be juxtaposed with all the consequential problems of the increasing demand for services and facilities in an economic and social climate in which funding has not kept pace. The remainder of this section looks at some specific provisions which may be associated with old age, although, of course, they may be relevant in the context of other sources of disability.

(2) Residential accommodation

Local authorities are empowered, and in terms of the 1968 Act, obliged, to provide residential accommodation in fulfillment of their statutory obligations, and this would include providing residential accommodation for persons who are elderly. Local authorities may not, however, provide residential accommodation with nursing. They can **arrange** for such accommodation, but it must be provided by someone other than the local authority.

Residential accommodation is increasingly provided by the private sector which has seen a major growth in the last ten to fifteen years. Private sector establishments may be purely residential, they may be nursing homes, or they may provide both personal care and nursing care. Residential homes must be registered with the local authority, which has powers of inspection and supervision. Nursing homes must be registered with the health board, which has powers of inspection and supervision. They differ from residential homes in that they provide nursing care. Finally, homes providing both types of care must register both with the local authority and with the health board.

All residential establishments are subject to local authority inspection. This process is likely to be extended from the present arms-length inspection of residential homes for persons who are elderly to the inspection of residential homes for children.

(3) Compulsory treatment

Section 47 of the National Assistance Act 1948 provides that treatment or other necessary care and attention can be given compulsorily to certain categories of people. The conditions which must be fulfilled before compulsory treatment can be contemplated are that the person concerned is unable to take proper care of him/herself and is not being properly cared for by anyone else **and** that **either** he/she is suffering from a grave chronic disease, **or** he/she is aged, infirm or physically incapacitated and living in insanitary conditions.

If these preconditions relating to inability to care for him/herself and disease/incapacity are fulfilled, proceedings can be started for the removal of the person concerned to hospital or some other suitable place (eg a residential or nursing home). The procedure is as follows:

(a) A certificate is obtained from the designated medical officer (DMO, designated by the health board) to the effect that he/she is satisfied that the person should be removed from the place where he/she is staying for one of the following reasons:
   (i) it is in the person's interest
   (ii) it is necessary to prevent injury to the health of others
   (iii) it is necessary for the prevention of a serious nuisance to other people.

(b) After the certificate is obtained the DMO or the local authority applies to the sheriff court for an order removing the person to a hospital or other suitable place. Normally seven days notice of the intention to make an application must be given to the person concerned. However, the requirement for notice can be dispensed with in emergencies if the DMO and another doctor certify that it is necessary in the person's interests that they be removed without delay. The DMO and any other doctor involved must attend court to give evidence in support of their certificates.

(c) The court may then grant the order sought. Before doing so the sheriff must be satisfied both as to the allegations contained in the certificate(s) and as to the desirability of making the order.

(d) Once granted, the order remains in force for the period specified in it, which can be up to three months, and can be extended for further periods of up to three months. An emergency order lasts initially for three weeks and can also be renewed.

(e) An application can be made to revoke an order, other than an emergency order, six weeks after the granting of the order.

This rather draconian procedure is not encountered often in practice, although it is used from time to time.

(4) Protection of property

Local authorities have a statutory duty[1] to take steps to protect the property of those who are admitted to hospital as patients, admitted to

1 National Assistance Act 1948, s48(2).

residential accommodation (whether provided by the authority or not), or subjected to compulsory treatment as described above. Where there is a danger of loss of or damage to the moveable property of such people and no other suitable arrangements have been made, the local authority must take reasonable steps to prevent or mitigate any loss or damage. In fulfilling this duty the authority is empowered to enter the person's usual residence and they can also recover any reasonable expenses.

(5) **Guardianship**

Guardianship has been considered more fully above (see part 5 above). The particular relevance of this to persons who are elderly is that dementia is a mental disorder which, if severe enough, could warrant the appointment of a guardian. The guardian has the power to decide where the patient should live and it has been pointed out that '... there has been a growing use of the procedure by social work departments to protect people suffering from dementia by ensuring their admission into residential care, which they are unwilling or unable to accept voluntarily.'[1] In most cases the guardian appointed is the social work department.

1 Blackie et al *Mental Health: A Guide to the Law in Scotland* (1990), p 32.

6. Offenders

1. LAW AND CRIME

As we noted in chapter 1, one of the principal functions of law is the maintenance of order in society. In turn, one of the main ways in which this is done is through the criminal law and the associated police, prosecution, court and other organisations. This chapter will look in more detail at the sentences available to courts and the roles that social workers play in the criminal justice system. Before doing this, however, we want to make some points which provide a context for the rest of the chapter.

Traditionally a link was made between crime and moral repugnance. Hume, for example, defined crime as, 'A doleful or wilful offence against society in the matter of violence, dishonesty, falsehood, irreligion.' With the passing of time and the growth in the number of offences this link has become weaker. It is difficult, unless an abstainer, to imagine that a substantial level of moral outrage is generated by the behaviour of someone who is drunk and incapable or of someone convicted of a minor breach of the peace. This is even clearer in the case of a large number of statutory offences. It is common, for example, for motoring offenders not to regard themselves as 'real' criminals.

Secondly, it should be noted that the majority of criminal offences in Scotland are the product of the common law; that is, their scope is determined by judicial decision rather than being defined in statute. This has further consequences. Firstly, aside from the limits set on the sentencing powers of particular courts, there is no limit on the sentence that can be imposed for common law crimes and offences. This is in contrast to statutory offences where, usually, the statute creating the offence will set a maximum penalty. Secondly, following from this, all common law crimes are potentially punishable by imprisonment. Thirdly, these crimes are subject to redefinition and refinement by the courts, with possible extension to cover novel circumstances. Recent examples of this include the extension of breach of the peace to cover a man dressed as a woman walking about in a red light district and the view of the High Court that selling what were effectively glue-sniffing kits amounted to 'a modern example of conduct which our law has for long regarded as criminal ... actions of any kind which cause or are a cause of real injury to the person'[1].

Thirdly, a distinction is sometimes drawn between crimes and offences (for example, in the presentation of criminal statistics) with the implication that crimes are more serious than offences. It is not clear that there is a sound legal basis for this, for example, the Criminal Procedure (Scotland) Act 1975 refers to murder as an offence.

Fourthly, some indication should be given of the balance of crime. In terms of reports of crime, the largest proportion are offences involving dishonesty, particularly theft, which usually account for about 40% of reports. Other significant contributors are miscellaneous offences, eg drunkenness, minor assault or breach of the peace, accounting for about 15% and motoring offences (30%); violent crimes are only 2% of the total. Looking at convictions, the largest contributor is motoring offences (over 30%), followed by miscellaneous offences (about 30%) and dishonesty (about 20%). Crimes of violence again account for about 2% of cases.

Finally, the issues relating to both women and black people and the law are especially significant for social workers. Clearly, the patterns of women's careers in the criminal justice system are very different from men's; the tariffs normally being higher and the custodial penalties being imposed sooner. Mary Eaton[2] asks 'Is it inevitable that the assumptions, language and practices of the courts and prisons reflect and reinforce the prevailing picture of women's "proper" and relatively powerless place in the social order?' To date little research has been published about the experience of black people in the Scottish criminal justice system, but the evidence of research in England suggests that black people are more likely to be imprisoned than white people and that police and victims may discriminate on the basis of perceived race. The presence of institutional racism as being 'built into the structure of society' is acknowledged by such writers as Alison Bowes and Duncan Sim[3] and as such will inevitably have implications for people's experience.

1 *Khaliq v HMA* 1984 SLT 137 at 142–3.
2 In *Gender, Crime and Justice* (1987), edited by Pat Carlen and Anne Worrall, p 100.
3 *Demands and Constraints – Ethnic Minorities and Social Services in Scotland* (1991).

2. SOCIAL WORK FUNCTIONS

Most of the social work functions in the criminal justice process are now covered by the *National Objectives and Standards for Social Work Services in the Criminal Justice System* issued in 1991 by the Scottish Office. These cover the provision of social enquiry reports and court based services, probation, throughcare, and community service. The *National Objectives* are associated with a change in the funding arrangements for financing social work services. Services in the areas covered are now 100% funded by central government. They are also associated with a change in the organisation of social work provision. These services are now mainly to be provided by specialist staff, some of whom will work full-time in this area.

The social worker performing any of the functions noted above will be accountable not only to the court but to his/her own employer. The differing value bases, policies and procedures will produce tensions which can sometimes escalate into conflicting demands being made upon the social worker. Involvement with the criminal justice system is likely to be stressful for everyone but especially so for the accused/offender/ex-offender who may be at risk of losing his/her liberty/money/other valued things. The structures and procedures of the criminal justice system are complex and can be particularly difficult to traverse for a person who is possibly in a state of crisis. In this situation, the social worker may contribute toward the alleviation of excessive anxiety and unclarity on the part of the accused/offender/ex-offender by taking on both a supportive and an educative role. As in many settings which are not primarily defined by social work values and knowledge, the social worker's most notable offering may be to help to broaden the perspective of all the players to include social factors.

(1) Court based social workers

There will be social work staff permanently based in larger, busier courts, while in other courts the provision may be part-time. The main functions of these court based social workers, as described in the *National Objectives*, are dealing with requests for social enquiry reports and ensuring that they are timeously provided, monitoring the standard of reports, conducting stand down interviews (in which the social worker interviews the offender during a brief court recess), and providing oral reports to the court, interviewing offenders immediately following a request for a report, interviewing offenders after custodial remand or sentence, interviewing offenders following sentences involving a social work contribution, and liaison with the others involved in the operation of the court.

Court based social workers not only perform a range of services for the court but may also be able to provide assistance to the families of those on trial or who have been sentenced, particularly those who have been sentenced to custody, and to victims of crime and witnesses. Here again, the social worker may be in a position to support and provide clarification about what is happening for the families of those appearing in court. In court when the disposal is pronounced, the offender may well be anxious and/or suffering from situational deafness and unable to hear and/or process what he/she hears. In many courts there is the added practical difficulty of physically hearing the disposal when there is no sound amplification and/or the crucial information is not clearly announced. Also many of the non-custodial disposals are not very widely used or known and so it may be necessary and appropriate for social workers to assume an educative and interpretive role with the offender in clarifying what the meaning and implications of various disposals are likely to be. In addition, the court based social worker may be providing an intake and referral service for those at the court who are in need.

(2) Social enquiry reports

Section 27 of the Social Work (Scotland) Act 1968 imposes a duty on local authority social work departments to 'provide reports relating to persons appearing before the court which the court may require for the disposal of the case.' Although the Act refers to social background reports, in the context of the criminal court system these reports are known as social enquiry reports. A detailed discussion of the contents of such reports and the methodology for preparing them is beyond the scope of this text and detailed guidelines and standards can be found in the *National Objectives*. Particularly in reports written about active/known social work department clients, it is hoped that there will be a strong element of a shared understanding of the problem areas with a commitment to the empowerment of the client.

Social enquiry reports **must** be obtained by courts before making a probation order or community service order, in the case of children under 16 appearing before the court, and in respect of someone under 18 who is subject to a supervision requirement from a children's hearing. In addition a court must obtain 'such information as it can about an offender's circumstances, character and physical and mental condition' before imposing the first sentence of imprisonment on an offender of 21 or over and before sentencing someone between 16 and

20 to detention. The normal mechanism for obtaining this information is the social enquiry report. Social workers have an opportunity to provide a concise but comprehensive systemic assessment which emphasises the social functioning equation for the court. It is crucial for the court to have access to information about the offender's normal coping capacities as well as the unusual environmental demands being made on the offender.

Normally the period available for preparation of the report will be 14 days when the offender has been remanded in custody; otherwise it is 21 days. These periods are reduced by the time taken to process the request and the need to complete the report to have it submitted to the clerk of court by midday on the day preceding the court hearing which will consider it. Where the offender is remanded on bail it is a condition of the bail that he/she co-operates in the preparation of any reports. Failure to co-operate should be reported to the court and is an offence[1].

A copy of the report is made available to the offender or his/her solicitor. It will also be seen by the prosecutor and the judge, and some comment may be made on its contents in open court. Because of this, problems about confidentiality may arise. Sensitive information may need to be noted as such in the report with a request that it is not disclosed, or it may be omitted from the report and brought to the attention of the judge in chambers in the presence of the offender and the defence agent.

The court may request that the writer is present at the hearing where the report will be presented to the court. Additionally, the *National Objectives* suggest that attendance is advisable where an unusual or complex recommendation is being made, where the writer's presence may tip the balance in favour of a non-custodial disposal, and where a report is being considered in connection with breach of a statutory order. In such cases the presence of the report writer may have a direct influence on the sentence passed. Where the writer is not present, a court based social worker may be able to assist the court on behalf of the writer.

Finally, it is worth noting that one of the objectives of social enquiry reports is variously stated to be '[t]o provide information and advice which may make it possible to increase the use of community based disposals where custody is likely', and 'assisting the court's consideration of community based options'. Part of the social worker's considerations are about the potential risk of the offender to him/herself and others in prison or in the community. In a Scotland where

1 See also ch 1, pt 10(5).

there is an acceptance that a sizeable proportion of persons currently in prison are no such risk to themselves or others, it is a rare and priceless opportunity for social workers to provide information to influence the sentencers to ends which are more compatible with social work values.

(3) Supervision

Social work departments are expected to provide supervision in a variety of situations. The main examples are probation, community services, fine supervision orders, supervised attendance orders and supervision after release from custody. These are all considered more fully below. Social workers may also be involved in diversion schemes, where alleged offenders are diverted into some form of social work intervention rather than being prosecuted, and this is also considered below.

(4) Appearing in court

Social workers are occasionally called as witnesses in civil or criminal proceedings and may also be the applicant in situations where there has been a breach of an order. In each of these situations, it is important that the social worker prepare thoroughly, bringing notes and copies of the relevant material to court. This last can be important as witnesses are allowed to refer to contemporaneous notes, ie notes made at the time of or shortly after the events to which they refer, while they are giving evidence.

Suggestions for social workers from Colin Fishwick in *Court Work*[1] include accommodating to the formal codes and norms of the court situation, being prepared to have one's practice exposed, preparing 'authoritative statements rather than interpretative remarks', direct and clear communication and appropriate style of dress. As this list suggests, court proceedings generally take place in a very formal atmosphere subject to detailed rules as to procedure[2] and as to how evidence may be given, and indeed what counts as evidence. This formality is reflected in the forms of address; magistrates are referred to as 'your honour', sheriffs and High Court judges as 'your lordship'. As regards evidence there is a general prohibition on opinion evidence with evidence generally expected to bring out the facts of the case.

1 2nd edn, 1989.
2 See ch 1, pt 10.

This rule against opinion evidence does not apply, however, where the witness giving evidence possesses a particular expertise. In such cases his/her opinion based on the application of that expertise to the facts is admissible.

(5) Court reports concerning children

When a child is charged with an offence which requires him/her to appear before the court[1], there is a requirement for the local authority to be notified. The social work department must then provide the court with a pre-conviction report detailing the home background and social circumstances of the child to facilitate disposal of the case[2].

3. SENTENCING: OBJECTIVES AND CRITERIA

The objectives of sentencing and punishment have produced a substantial literature. The main objectives canvassed in the past have included: individual and general deterrence, rehabilitation or reform, retribution, denunciation, and containment or protection of the public. The extent to which the sentences available to the courts can meet any of these objectives is increasingly open to doubt. For example, it is debatable whether the element of calculation required for deterrence to operate is present in most crimes; the possibility of reforming someone and preparing them for a life integrated in society by isolating them in prison is equally debatable. The only objectives that the system can be said to attain are retribution and denunciation, with, in some cases compensation for the victim of crime, and, in other cases the possibility of some reformation. This, indeed, was recognised in the White Paper *Crime, Justice and Protecting the Public*[3], which also contained the novel suggestion that the objective of sentencing was ensuring that criminals received their just desserts.

On a more practical level there are factors which clearly have an influence on the sentence imposed in particular cases. These include the severity of the offence, the offender's previous record, his/her attitude towards the offence, the offender's culpability, the existence of any provocation, and background information about the offender. In contrast to the position in England, however, there is no discount

1 See ch 4, pt 4(3).
2 Criminal Procedure (Scotland) Act 1975, ss40, 308.
3 Cm 965 (1990).

on sentence for a plea of guilty. On the basis of these factors experienced practitioners, on both sides of the law, can often predict the likely outcome of a particular case.

Although these factors exist, and have to some extent been given judicial recognition, there is some evidence of disparities in sentencing between different courts and between different judges.

In practice the vast majority of sentences are non-custodial. In 1990, for example, just over 7% of those sentenced were sentenced to custody. It should be noted, however, that the use of custody is increasing; in 1979 this figure was just over 4%.

4. NON-CUSTODIAL DISPOSALS

(1) Absolute discharge

An absolute discharge is appropriate where in view of the circumstances, including the nature of the offence and the character of the offender, the court decides that it is inexpedient to inflict punishment and that a probation order is not appropriate. It is used very rarely and in 1990 was used in only 0.4% of cases. This disposal is regarded as an order rather than a sentence and so will not count as a previous conviction unless there is a further offence committed subsequently.

(2) Admonition

An offender may be admonished where it appears to meet the justice of the case. The court may simply announce that the offender is admonished and leave it at that, or the court may direct some well chosen words of warning at him/her. This disposal counts as a conviction.

(3) Caution[1]

The offender may be required to find caution for his/her good behaviour. This involves him/her lodging a sum of money in court. The period of good behaviour may be up to six months in the district court, up to 12 months in the sheriff summary court and for statutory offences tried on indictment, otherwise there is no maximum. The

1 Pronounced 'kayshun'.

maximum amounts of caution which can be required are currently £2,500 for district courts, £5,000 in the sheriff summary court and otherwise unlimited. If the offender is not of good behaviour during the period, this usually involves commission of a further offence, then the caution is forfeited.

(4) Fines

This disposal takes the form of a financial penalty paid by the offender. Since fines are by far the commonest form of disposal and consistently account for about 80% of disposals, it is vital for social workers to appreciate how they are levied and collected. Social workers also play a central role in the preparation of means enquiry reports for the court[1].

(a) Levels of fine

In fixing the level of fine for a particular offender the court must, among other considerations, take the means of the offender into account; there is clearly little point in levying a fine which the offender has no practical prospect of paying. Here, the social worker who is asked to prepare a social enquiry report is ideally placed to help to minimise the prospect of an unpayable fine being levied by providing the sentencer with comprehensive and accurate information about the financial incomings and outgoings of the offender.

In the case of both common law and statutory offences tried on indictment, there is no maximum limit on the fine which can be imposed. In summary courts there are limits. For common law offences these are currently £5,000 in the sheriff court and for stipendiary magistrates, and £2,500 for lay magistrates in the district court. In the case of statutory offences the statute creating the offence will normally fix the maximum fine, and this will be done by reference to one of five levels, rather than by reference to an amount of money. The reason for this is simple; it is much easier to change the values attached to the levels rather than having to amend the amounts stated in a large, and growing, number of Acts of Parliament. Currently the levels are as follows:

Level 1 £200
Level 2 £500
Level 3 £1,000

1 *See below.*

Level 4 £2,500
Level 5 £5,000

It should be noted that the maximum fine that can be levied by lay magistrates in the district court is stated to be Level 4 and the money value will therefore change automatically when the levels change.

(b) *Time for payment*

The offender must be allowed at least seven days to pay the fine, or if it is to be paid in instalments, the first instalment of the fine. The only exceptions to this, when the fine is payable immediately, are: where the offender has no fixed abode, where the offender appears to have sufficient means to pay the fine forthwith, where the offender indicates that he/she does not want time to pay, and where the court is satisfied that other special reasons exist for not allowing time to pay.

The offender may, either when the fine is imposed or subsequently, apply for more time to pay or to be allowed to pay by instalments. Further time to pay must be allowed following an application unless it appears that the offender's failure to pay is wilful or that there is no reasonable prospect of him/her paying the fine. Social workers may find that the role of advocate on behalf of their clients in negotiating for a feasible instalment schedule would be appropriate, since offenders often experience difficulty in overcoming their inhibitions in the courtroom or with the clerk of the relevant court to make such arrangements.

(c) *Alternative of imprisonment*

An alternative sentence of imprisonment may be imposed at the same time as the fine and will become operational without the need for a means enquiry court (see (e) below) in the event of default in payment. Such an alternative is not to be imposed unless the court considers it expedient having regard to the gravity of the offence, character of the offender or other special circumstances.

(d) *Fine supervision*

In cases where an offender is given time to pay or payment is to be by instalments the offender may be made subject to a fine supervision order and be placed under the supervision of a social worker or other social work department employee. The offender does not need to consent to such an order being made and the order remains in force until the fine is paid in full, the offender is imprisoned for fine default, another order is made concerning the fine, or the order is transferred to another court area. An offender under 21 cannot be detained in the event of non-payment unless he/she has been placed on supervision or it was not reasonably practicable to do this. In the event of non-payment the supervising social worker should provide a report to the court hearing called to enquire as to the reasons for non-payment (the means enquiry court, see below). There have been arguments advanced over the years that supervising the payment of fines places social workers in an unacceptable position as debt collectors for the courts, but compulsory contact between the offender and the social worker does offer the potential opportunity for more substantive and negotiated work to be undertaken together.

(e) Enforcement: imprisonment on default

Generally speaking fines are enforced by the courts which imposed them. The exceptions to this are High Court fines, which are enforced by the appropriate sheriff court, and cases where the offender has moved. In the latter case the fine will normally be transferred to the appropriate court covering the offender's new place of residence.

If the offender fails to pay his/her fine he/she may be imprisoned instead. Where time to pay has been allowed and no alternative imposed at the time of the fine, imprisonment can only take place after enquiry by the court as to the reasons for non-payment. The hearing at which this enquiry is made is usually referred to as a means enquiry court. At this hearing the offender may be imprisoned or given further time to pay. There is statutory provision for the period of imprisonment in the event of non-payment. At the moment this ranges from seven days for a fine of up to £200 to ten years for a fine in excess of £1 million. The relevant amount for the purpose of calculating the period of imprisonment is the amount of the fine which remains outstanding. The same provisions apply, subject to the proviso noted above, for the imposition of an alternative of detention on a young offender.

Where no time to pay is allowed and the offender does not make immediate payment he/she may, subject to the exception noted below, be committed to prison/young offender institution forthwith. The exception arises in the case of an offender who has not previously served a term of imprisonment/detention and who is not legally represented. Such an offender cannot be immediately imprisoned unless he/she has been refused legal aid on financial grounds or, knowing of the possibility of applying for legal aid, he/she has chosen not to apply for it.

In these instances, a person can be imprisoned for an offence which did not originally carry imprisonment as a possible penalty and for an offence for which prison had not been envisioned as a possible penalty. A substantial proportion of Scotland's prisoners are fine defaulters. In 1990 about 40% of sentenced prisoners received into prison were fine defaulters.

If the fine is paid while the offender is in prison for fine default, then his/her release can be secured. Young offenders who have outstanding fines and are imprisoned for other offences may apply through the governor of the institution to the Secretary of State for any outstanding fines to be remitted.

(f) *Supervised attendance orders*

These were instituted by the Law Reform (Miscellaneous Provisions)(Scotland) Act 1990, and were introduced experimentally in May 1992 in South Ayrshire and in June 1992 in Highland and Tayside Regions. Supervised attendance orders give courts an alternative to imprisonment in the event of non-payment.

Supervised attendance orders can be used where, but for their existence, an offender over the age of 16 would have been imprisoned/detained as a result of default and provided the court considers a supervised attendance order more appropriate than imprisonment. The court must also have been notified that arrangements for supervised attendance exist in the area.

The order requires the offender to attend at a place of supervision for a specified number of hours which may be 10, 20, 30, 40, 50 or 60. The attendance should normally be completed within 12 months. A social worker will be appointed to supervise the offender, and the offender must report any change of address or change of times of employment to the supervising officer. The offender must also comply with instructions given by the supervising officer, and these must, so far as practicable, avoid conflict with the offender's religious beliefs and interference with his/her employment or education.

Breaches of the order are reported to court. If the court is satisfied that the offender has failed to comply with the order without reasonable cause it may revoke the order and impose the alternative of imprisonment dictated by the outstanding amount of fine or it may vary the number of hours, provided the total does not exceed 60.

The offender or supervisor may apply to court for the order to be extended beyond the normal 12 months, for the number of hours to be varied, for revocation, and for revocation and the imposition of imprisonment. The court should grant such an application if it appears to them that 'it would be in the interests of justice to do so having regard to circumstances which have arisen since the order was made'.

There is also provision for transfer of orders where the offender moves and arrangements exist in the new area for supervised attendance.

(5) Probation

(a) Introduction

Probation is a disposal that requires the offender to be under the supervision of a professionally qualified social worker who is appointed as his/her supervisor for a period between six months and three years. The offender must comply with the instructions of the supervisor and with any conditions attached to the supervision order. In summary courts (except where it is imposed following a deferred sentence) a probation order will be made before conviction, in solemn courts it follows conviction. A court may deal with an offender by way of probation if 'it is of the opinion having regard to the circumstances, including the nature of the offence and the character of the offender' that it is expedient to do so. The *National Objectives* suggest that priority should be given in recommending probation to two groups: (i) offenders whose current offending places them at risk of custody, who have significant underlying problems and who seem likely to re-offend; and (ii) repeat offenders with significant underlying problems who are at risk of custody, even if the current offence is trivial. They also suggest some priority for offenders who may be likely to receive a custodial disposal if their offending behaviour continues unchecked.

Before a probation order is made the court must obtain a social enquiry report. If the writer of the report is recommending probation, the report should also detail the action plan to be followed during the probation period and any special conditions which should be attached to the order. The offender must consent to the making of a probation order, and part of the social work function in preparing the report involves explaining the consequences of a probation order to the offender and obtaining his/her consent to the order. The court must also explain the meaning and effect of the order and the consequences of breach of conditions of the order or commission of a further offence. Copies of the order must be supplied to the offender and to the supervising social worker.

Once the order has been made, the supervising social worker should see the probationer within a week, giving him/her a copy of the order and having the signing of that order by the probationer witnessed. The signing is taken to be the evidence that the probationer understands the meaning and conditions of the order. In the event of subsequent breach proceedings, failure to complete this procedure might provide the probationer with grounds to contest the proceedings.

The probation order can be used to confront the offender with the consequences of his/her offending behaviour by placing various restrictions on his/her activities, as the basis for identifying and resolving some of the problems which led him/her into offending behaviour, as a means of working with offenders toward a clearer and more acceptable understanding of his/her place in society and as a credible alternative to the court in controlling and providing an opportunity for the offender to help him/herself. Once more, the social worker is well placed to begin the process of problem solving with the offender. The social workers care/control dichotomy/dilemma is probably nowhere more evident than in this relationship. A detailed discussion of the contradictory demands made of supervisors of probation orders can be found elsewhere.[1]

Detailed guidelines for the frequency and the content of contact through the initial, middle and final phases of the probation are available in the *National Objectives*.

(b) Conditions

There are certain standard or core conditions which apply to all probation orders. These are that the offender is to be of good behaviour, that he/she is to comply with instructions given by the supervising officer, and that the offender must inform his/her supervisor at once of any change of address or employment.

In addition to these core conditions there are others envisaged and provided for in the legislation. These are: as to residence, as to performance of unpaid work, requiring the payment of compensation to the victim of the offence, requiring security to be found for good behaviour, and requiring medical treatment for mental illness. Each of these will be considered in turn in the following paragraphs.

A requirement requiring residence can take two forms: it can require the offender to reside at a named place or in a named institution, or it can require that the offender's place of residence is approved by his/her supervisor. In the former case the requirement can last for up to 12 months from the making of the order.

1 Eg Tim May in *Probation: Politics, Policy and Practice* (1990) or John Rodger in 'Social work as social control re-examined: beyond the dispersal of discipline thesis', in *Sociology* 22(4).

The performance of unpaid work can be made a condition of a probation order where the offender has committed an offence punishable by imprisonment and where he/she is at serious risk of a custodial sentence. As we have already noted, the first of these requirements is not very restrictive as all common law crimes and offences are potentially punishable by imprisonment. The minimum period of work is 40 hours and the maximum 240 hours.

Although a compensation order (see below) cannot be made at the same time as a probation order, it is possible to make payment of compensation a condition of a probation order. The supervisor has responsibility for supervising the payment of compensation into court.

Lodging of a sum of money for up to 12 months as security for good behaviour may also be made a condition of probation. The security will be forfeited in the event of breach of the requirement for good behaviour, otherwise it is returned, with interest, at the end of the period specified.

Treatment for mental disorder can be made a condition of a probation order where the court is satisfied that the offender suffers from a mental condition which requires and may be susceptible to treatment, but that the mental condition is not such as to justify the making of a hospital order (see below). The court can make this decision on the basis of the evidence of a registered medical practitioner. The probation condition may require treatment as an in-patient, as an out-patient, or by a named doctor for up to 12 months from the date of the order. It may be amended to allow for better or more convenient treatment and the court must be informed of the discontinuation of treatment. Where the requirement is for in-patient treatment the role of the supervisor may well be restricted.

Finally, as well as these conditions which the legislation specifically provides for, the social worker may recommend and the court may impose any other condition which it considers to be conducive to securing the good conduct of the offender and preventing him/her from re-offending. Examples of such conditions include refraining from association with known offenders/ex-offenders, refraining from specified behaviours like drinking, or participating in identified therapeutic programmes.

(c) *Amendment and discharge of order*

The order may be amended on the application of the offender or the supervisor. Any amendment cannot reduce the period of probation or extend it beyond the three year maximum and cannot extend the period of residence in a named place or of medical treatment beyond 12 months from the date the order was originally made.

If the offender moves application may be made for transfer of the order to the new area either by the offender or by the supervisor. If the application is made by the supervisor the court must grant the application.

Either the probationer or the supervisor may apply for discharge of the order. The *National Objectives* suggest that the possibility of application for discharge should be considered halfway through the order and at subsequent reviews.

(d) *Breach of order: failure to comply with conditions*

Where the offender breaches any of the requirements of the order, for example by unsatisfactory performance of work or failure to comply with instructions of his/her supervisor, breach proceedings before the court may be initiated. In deciding whether or not to initiate proceedings the supervisor should consider the seriousness of the breach and the reasonableness of the explanation for it offered by the offender. The *National Objectives* suggest that less serious cases should be dealt with by way of a formal warning, with the proviso that after two warnings the breach procedure should be initiated. Since there is some discretion in this process, it is imperative that social workers and their managers have considered and agreed criteria for the decisions taken. Clearly, these decisions are not taken lightly since the liberty of an individual is in jeopardy and so it is imperative that there be an internal logic and consistency. This is unfortunately also necessary in view of a history of some social worker's therapeutic optimism and/or over-identification with the client.

Breach proceedings are initiated by the supervisor applying to the court for a breach of probation. It is then up to the court to decide whether to take action against the offender. If it does, the breach must be sworn to by the supervisor. The court may then issue a warrant for the arrest of the offender or cite him/her to attend court. The precise details as to how breach proceedings are initiated will be the subject of local agreements.

If the breach is proved or admitted the court may: impose a fine up to Level 3 (currently £1,000); revoke the order and sentence the offender for the original offence; vary the conditions attached to the order, providing that this does not extend the order beyond three years; or, continue the order and impose, in addition, a community service order (CSO). Before this last option can be used the preconditions for imposing a CSO must be fulfilled (see below).

(e) *Breach of order: commission of further offence*

When an offender on probation commits a further offence during the life of the order breach proceedings should always be initiated. In this case the powers of the court are to continue the probation order or to impose sentence for the original offence.

(6) Community service

(a) Introduction

A community service order requires the offender to perform between 40 and 240 hours of unpaid work. The sentence should normally be completed within 12 months. Before a CSO is used in a particular case the court must have obtained a social enquiry report which includes an assessment of the offender's suitability for the community service scheme and of the suitability of the work available to him/her. In producing this report the community service scheme (ie the body which administers community service; providing and supervising placements) must be consulted and the writer of the report should explain to the offender what a CSO involves so that he/she is in a position to consent to it.

The expectation is that community service orders will be used **only** as an alternative to imprisonment or detention; in other words they should be used only where the alternative is a custodial disposal and never as a net widener. Legislation making this a legal requirement is on the statute book but has not yet been brought into effect.

(b) The order

In making the order the court must explain the purpose and effect of the order, the consequences of failure to comply with it, and the court's power to revoke and amend the order at the instance either of the offender or his/her supervisor. The consent of the offender to the order must be obtained and the order must specify the number of hours to be worked.

Following sentence the offender will be seen by a community service officer who will be employed by the social work department but may not be a qualified social worker. The community service officer will allocate him/her to a work placement and be responsible for his/her supervision during the life of the order. There is a statutory requirement to avoid conflict as far as practicable with the offender's religious beliefs and his/her employment or education. In addition, other factors are clearly relevant, for example any impairment or skills. Typically the work will be in painting/decorating, gardening, cleaning/kitchen work or in sports/youth clubs. Occasionally the work will provide opportunities to the offender to learn new skills.

Appropriate performance and behaviour standards will be set at the outset and work placements must be closely monitored to ensure that these are met.

The offender must notify the supervisor at once of any change of address or change in the times when he/she works.

(c) Breach

The procedures to be followed in the event of breach are considered in detail in the *National Objectives*. These envisage, in serious cases, a three stage process of formal warning, final warning and breach proceedings. At the final stage an application is made to court to institute breach proceedings. The application must be accompanied by a report from the community service officer and then it is up to the court to decide on the institution of proceedings. If the breach is admitted or established the court may: continue the order with the possible addition of a fine up to Level 3 (currently £1,000); vary the number of hours, provided that the total does not exceed 240; or, revoke the order and sentence the offender for the original offence. Since a CSO is only to be used in cases where otherwise a custodial disposal would be used, it will almost certainly be the case that the alternative sentence will be custodial.

(d) Revocation, amendment and transfer

Either the supervisor or the offender may apply for revocation or amendment of the order, and the court must grant the application if it appears to be in the interests of justice to do so having regard to changes in circumstances since the order was made. Examples would include prolonged illness or change in the offender's employment situation. The amendment may be to alter the number of hours or to extend the 12 month period in which the work is to be completed. In the case of revocation the court may simply revoke the order, or may revoke the order and substitute another sentence.

Where the offender moves and there are facilities for community service in the new area, he/she or the supervisor may apply for a transfer of the order to the new area. If the application is made by the supervisor the court must grant the application.

(7) Compensation order

Compensation orders were introduced by the Criminal Justice (Scotland) Act 1980. This disposal counts as a sentence when convictions are libelled. Courts have the power to grant compensation orders up to the amount of the maximum fine which they can levy. The compensation order is designed to compensate the victim for any personal injury, loss or damage caused to them by the offender. In making a compensation order the court must take into account the means of the offender and so here again it is vital that any social enquiry report include accurate and comprehensive information about the offender's income and expenses. Where the offender's means are not sufficient to pay both a fine and a compensation order the latter should be preferred. The compensation order may be imposed in addition to as well as instead of other penalties.

The provisions for review, remission and enforcement of compensation orders are similar to those considered above for fines, though, in addition, review may be sought where the victim's loss turns out to be less than it appeared at the time of the order.

Payment of the sum ordered is made to the clerk of court who passes it on to the victim. Payments made by the offender will be counted towards a compensation order before any fine made at the same time.

The making of a compensation order will not affect the victim's ability to raise a civil action for damages against the offender or to claim under the criminal injuries compensation scheme (see below). In either case, however, the amount of a compensation order will be deducted from any award made to the victim.

(8) Deferred sentence

This is not strictly a disposal, but amounts to the court deferring sentence for a period of time. In the majority of cases when it is used, sentence will be deferred so that reports can be obtained on the offender. In other cases sentence may be deferred for a longer period, for example 3, 6 or 12 months for other purposes. A court may defer sentence, for example, for the offender to be of good behaviour during the period of deferment or to allow the offender to make reparation to the victim. In such cases the expectation is that if the condition attached to the deferment is fulfilled a lesser sentence will be imposed than otherwise. Where sentence is deferred in a case where a social enquiry report has been prepared, the court will often ask for a supplementary report to be prepared for the deferred hearing.

If the offender commits another offence during the period of deferment he/she may be brought before the court for sentence without waiting for the deferred date.

The time of deferral can be used constructively by the social worker and offender to identify and explore problem areas and evaluate the potential effectiveness of various disposals. Although sentence can be deferred, there is no provision such as exists in England and Wales for sentences to be suspended. Unlike a deferred sentence a suspended sentence involves the imposition of a sentence of detention, the effect of which is suspended for a fixed period and will only be served if the offender commits a further offence punishable by imprisonment during that period.

5. DIVERSION FROM PROSECUTION

(1) Conditional offers of fixed penalties

(a) Criminal Justice (Scotland) Act 1987, section 56

This provision allows a procurator fiscal to make a conditional offer of a fixed penalty in the case of any offence which could be prosecuted in the district court, subject to the general exclusion of motoring offences. If the offer is accepted no proceedings will be taken against the alleged offender and no conviction will be recorded. In the event that the offer is accepted and the alleged offender then defaults, recovery of the remainder of the penalty is by way of civil diligence. Apart from that many of the provisions applicable to fine recovery apply, so that enforcement must be preceded by a means enquiry court and the individual could be placed on supervision until the penalty is paid.

These provisions have been used quite extensively, mostly for breach of the peace. About 80% of offers have been accepted, with most of the remainder prosecuted[1]. These measures do, however raise a number of questions about rights of individuals to have their guilt or innocence established.

(b) Road Traffic Offenders Act 1988

This legislation allows the procurator fiscal to make a conditional offer of a fixed penalty in respect of a number of motoring offences. The procedure is similar to that outlined above.

1 Scottish Office Statistical Bulletin *Criminal Proceedings in Scottish Courts 1990*, CRJ 1992/3, 22.

(2) Social work diversion

There are a number of diversion schemes operating in Scotland which involve social work input. They generally involve diversion before prosecution. In other words the person involved accepts some appropriate form of social work intervention, eg to tackle an alcohol problem, as an alternative to prosecution. In some schemes the acceptance of social work intervention will mean that no prosecution will take place while in others the decision not to prosecute is taken after assessing the outcome of the diversion. Questions abound concerning the difficulty of getting informed consent by the person either threatened with prosecution or having already begun the process of being prosecuted.

Individuals will normally be assessed by the social work department before being accepted for diversion. The role of the social worker is complex and contradictory in respect to this task in that he/she is responsible for data collection and analysis under what are probably very stressful circumstances, for explaining the procedure to the client, and for offering other appropriate social work services in supporting the client and his/her family through what may well be a crisis. The existence of these schemes raises a number of important issues including concerns about 'net widening'. In other words the possibility that the existence of the scheme leads to intervention where previously there would have been no prosecution, or a warning letter would have been sent, and concerns about the types of case where diversion is appropriate, the most contentious being violent assault in the family.

6. COMPENSATION FOR CRIMINAL INJURIES

People who suffer personal injury as a result of violent crimes are entitled to claim compensation under the criminal injuries compensation scheme, which is administered by the criminal injuries compensation board (CICB). Any award can include an element for *solatium*, ie the pain and suffering caused by the injury, and for any financial loss, eg loss of earnings, resulting from the injury. Claims which would result in an award of less than £1,000 will not be entertained.

One area of recent interest is the possibility of claiming compensation for child abuse. In some cases, those where the child concerned is in care, the social work department may be directly involved in assisting a child to make a claim under the scheme. In child abuse cases an award will only be made if certain requirements are fulfilled.

Firstly, in cases where the victim and person responsible for the injury were living in the same household there must have been a prosecution of the person responsible or good reasons for no prosecution. Secondly, the guilty party must not benefit from the award (as might happen if victim and perpetrator were once again in the same household). Thirdly, making an award must not be against the child's interests. Substantial awards made to children will generally be managed by the CICB until the child is 18, except where the child is in care where the expectation is that the award will be administered by the social work department.

7. CUSTODIAL DISPOSALS

(1) Imprisonment

Imprisonment is a disposal only available for those aged 21 or over. Where an offender has not previously been sentenced to imprisonment or detention the court cannot impose a sentence of imprisonment (except the mandatory life sentence for murder) without first considering information regarding the offender's character, circumstances and physical and mental condition (usually provided in a social enquiry report); in addition the court must consider that no other disposal is appropriate and, if it is a summary court, must state and record the reason for this opinion.

The maximum length of sentence may be restricted in the case of a statutory offence by the statute creating it. In other cases the limit will be the maximum sentence the court can impose. In the case of lay magistrates this is 60 days. For stipendiary magistrates and the sheriff summary court the limit is three months, except where the conviction is for a crime of violence or dishonesty and there is a previous conviction for a cognate offence; here the maximum is six months. The sheriff solemn court can imprison for up to three years, and has the power, rarely used, to remit a case to the High Court for sentence where its powers are inadequate. There is no limit on the period of imprisonment that can be imposed by the High Court.

Where an offender is convicted of two or more offences, sentences of imprisonment may be imposed which are concurrent or consecutive; if the latter, the terms of imprisonment follow on from each other. Courts' powers to impose consecutive sentences may be limited by their maximum sentencing powers, eg a sheriff sitting in a summary court could not normally impose consecutive sentences which, when added together, exceeded three months. This limitation will **not** apply where the convictions are on separate complaints/ indictments and arise from distinct incidents.

Prisoners serving a sentence of more than five days may be granted remission of up to one third of their sentence, provided the remaining period exceeds five days[1].

It is generally agreed that it is hard to justify the present extent of the use of custodial measures in Scotland. As argued earlier, it is mainly ineffective and it is very expensive compared to any other alternative. Social workers have a special opportunity particularly in the current climate to develop credible alternatives and to publicise these options to sentencers; indeed, as we have seen, this is the perspective adopted by the *National Objectives*.

The law relating to release on parole is dealt with in part 8 below.

(2) Detention of young offenders

Offenders between 16 and 20 may be sentenced to detention in a young offender institution. Previously offenders in this age group could be sentenced to borstal training or to detention in a detention centre; these options are no longer available. Young offenders are incarcerated in separate institutions from adult offenders and there is a greater emphasis, where possible, on high standards of discipline and training. Reconviction rates and recidivism remain very high. Before sentencing an offender to detention the court must consider the same information as is appropriate in the case of an offender of 21 and over who is sentenced to his/her first term of imprisonment. The court must also be of the opinion, based on this information, that no other way of dealing with the offender is appropriate and, except for the High Court, record the reason for this opinion. Offenders aged between 18 and 21 who are convicted of murder will be sentenced to detention for life.

The same rules as to remission apply as to prison sentences. Parole and post-release supervision are considered in part 8 below.

(3) Detention of children[2]

A child under the age of 18 who is convicted of murder is to be detained without limit of time in conditions specified by the Secretary of State. Children under 16 convicted in a solemn court may be

1 See pt 8(4) below for proposed changes.
2 See also ch 4, pt 5.

sentenced to detention, again in conditions determined by the Secretary of State[1]. Summary courts may impose sentences of detention in residential care for up to 12 months on offenders under 16 and in this case the care is provided by the relevant local authority[2]. Absconders subject to such sentences must be returned to the named establishments by the police.

The children's hearing will normally have had some involvement in such cases in providing consultation and advice. Social workers must ask if the child in question is a danger to him/herself or others and must attempt to present this and other relevant information to the sentencers.

(4) Social work in prison

There are local authority social workers based in the prisons in Scotland with the general remit of providing a social work service to prisoners in need. The overwhelming fact of life for this work is that security is the primary objective of the host institution and all other considerations are subject to directives arising out of that factor. This manifests itself in practical problems – amongst others about: arranging to interview prisoners; arranging for 'welfare visits' for prisoners with their families; communicating information to prisoners and receiving information from prisoners; prison regimes restricting the time, timing and place for interviews. Other problems include working with the possibly very different value base, attitudes and assumptions of prison staff, working within an extremely hierarchically organised institution, working within the restrictions imposed by the Official Secrets Act, and possibly working with one member of a family system which has been broken apart.

There are also extraordinary opportunities potentially available to social workers in prison, as anyone who has worked with people in crisis and with a high level of motivation will know. At the time of entry and just before release from prison it is likely that the prisoner will demonstrate a drive to solve problems caused by his/her imprisonment, resolve difficulties which led to offending behaviour, and lay the groundwork for returning to live in the community.

In recent years, social workers in prisons have initiated the development of a whole range of innovatory services and programmes including working with those who have sexually abused children, who have

1 Criminal Procedure (Scotland) Act 1975, s206.
2 Ibid, s413, as amended by the Criminal Justice (Scotland) Act 1987.

acknowledged problems with substance abuse, who had been homeless, and who have mental health problems. As other long-stay institutions decrease in size and close, it is clear that more people who previously had been in such total institutions are finding their way into the prisons and social workers in prison will be increasingly called upon to provide a wider range of services to meet these people's needs.

8. PAROLE AND AFTERCARE

(1) Prisoners and young offenders

Parole, introduced in 1967, has been welcomed by most as part of an attempt to relieve some of the prison overcrowding and introduce a more civil liberties oriented approach to prisoners. There are others, however, who are concerned that the measures do not go nearly far enough and about the lack of supervision for newly released ex-prisoners in the community.

The practicalities of parole are that those sentenced to terms of imprisonment or detention can be considered for release on licence after serving one third of their sentence or 12 months, whichever is the longer. In practice this restriction, combined with the effects of remission, mean that parole only affects those serving sentences of more than 18 months. There are further restrictions in that those sentenced to more than five years for violent crimes will not be released more than a few months (up to eight) before they would otherwise be released at the end of their sentence. In addition those convicted of terrorist offences will not be released on parole.

The prison or young offender institution will be informed of the prisoner's eligibility for parole some time in advance of the date when he/she qualifies for release. At this stage the prisoner will be asked if he/she wishes to be considered for parole and may indicate that this is not desired. For those prisoners (over 90%) who do wish to be considered a dossier is prepared. Among the contents of this will be a home circumstances report, prepared by a social worker in the area where the prisoner intends to reside on release and a report prepared by a prison social worker. The objectives and contents of these reports are detailed in the *National Objectives*.

The ideal model for the compiling of these reports would be if the field social worker who wrote the original social enquiry report for the court, if one was required, or who has been working with the family of the prisoner and has maintained a through-care contact with the prisoner is the person who now completes the home circumstances report. The prison social worker who has been working with the prisoner in resolving some of the problems associated with his/her imprisonment would ideally be the one to write the other report. Difficulties typically arise when there has been a break in the contact between the prisoner and the person/s with whom he/she proposes to live and/or misunderstandings have arisen between these parties. After all, families have learned to live without the prisoner and may appreciate the contribution of a social worker in helping them to clarify their thoughts and feelings about the prisoner's impending return to the community.

The dossier then goes to the local review committee for the institution where the prisoner is detained for their consideration. If they do not recommend parole then, unless the case is referred to the parole board by officials in the Scottish Office Home and Health Department (SOHHD), the prisoner will not be paroled. Negative recommendations referred by the SOHHD officials, positive recommendations and split decisions are referred to the parole board for Scotland for a recommendation, which the Secretary of State will normally follow in granting/refusing parole. If parole is refused the prisoner's case will normally be reviewed in 12 months. The process of application for parole can be enormously stressful for both the prisoner and his/her family and the support and advice of the social worker may be most welcome and needed.

If parole is granted the prisoner is released on a licence which will, in practice, remain in force until the two-thirds stage of his/her sentence (ie the time when release with full remission would take place) has been reached. There are standard conditions attached to the licence which can be added to by the parole board. The main conditions are a requirement to submit to social work supervision, to be of good behaviour and keep the peace, and to obtain the prior permission of the supervisor before travelling abroad. The conditions in an existing licence can be varied by the parole board and supervisors may apply for such variation.

Social work with a parolee is as geared to the comprehensive systemic assessment of the individual and his/her situation as any other social work. There are, however, several special areas which must be considered. These include helping the parolee to make sense of his/her new living environment which may have altered considerably in his/her absence. Practical problems usually take centre stage initially – arranging for the payment of income maintenance from the Department of Social Security and finding accommodation. Relationships with others may have been strained beyond reparation while others may require much effort and understanding to rejuvenate. Finding work may be especially difficult. Parolees are generally very vulnerable to the problems associated with mass unemployment and deprivation and unless some of the problems which resulted in offending behaviour have been outgrown or resolved, they are likely to resurface relatively quickly. Here the support and guidance of a social worker can be invaluable.

In practice revocation of the licence and recall to prison is initiated by the supervisor, who has some discretion in deciding whether or not to initiate this process. A report from the supervisor will be considered by the parole board which makes a recommendation to the Secretary of State. In some cases the case will be dealt with by way of a warning letter, but in others the parolee will be recalled to custody. On recall the parolee has a statutory right to make representations to the parole board, which may order his/her re-release. In practice recalls are referred to the parole board whether or not the parolee makes representations. Courts also have power to revoke a licence in the event of commission of a further offence, but this power is very rarely used. Again, the *National Objectives* document outlines detailed guidance on the criteria for social workers making decisions regarding the initiation of proceedings.

In the case of young offenders there are additional provisions under which they may be required to be subject to supervision on release. In the case of release on licence the supervision is to continue for 12 months or the duration of the licence, if longer. In other cases where the sentence exceeded 6 months, the maximum period of supervision will be 6 months if the sentence was less than 18 months and 12 months otherwise. Application can be made to SOHHD for early termination of this requirement. Social work involvement with young offenders may be especially significant in respect of the developmental stage and tasks for the young person returning to the community. Typically, a young person's drive toward identity and independence will have been curtailed while institutionalised and upon release he/she may be hurled back into the family home through lack of other suitable accommodation. He/she may have very poor educational attainments, qualifications and previous work experience which will pose further impediments upon resettlement. While clearly no panacea, social work involvement through counselling and support may well be crucial in enabling the young person to make positive choices for the future.

(2) Prisoners serving life sentences

In these cases an initial decision will be taken by a body known as the preliminary review committee as to when the prisoner will first be reviewed for parole. After this the procedure for review again involves the local review committee and the parole board, but reference will also be made to the Lord Justice-General and the trial judge. If release is not recommended there is no automatic right to annual review. If release is recommended the prisoner will go through a pre-release programme. In life cases the licence remains in force for the duration of the parolee's life, and the provisions for recall and re-release are the same as those noted above. In certain cases, for example murders of police officers, sexual or sadistic child murders and murders by firearm in the course of a crime, release will not usually be contemplated before 20 years. Here again, the process of applying for parole may be extraordinarily stressful and frightening for the prisoner and for his/her family and the support and guidance of a social worker may be useful. Once released, the burden for the parolee and family of living with the sword of Damocles hanging relentlessly over their heads must be acknowledged and worked with.

(3) Release of children

(a) Children detained after sentence on indictment

Such children can be released by the Secretary of State on licence, with the proviso that if the sentence exceeds 18 months the parole board must have recommended release. The licence will remain in force for 12 months or until the **end** of the sentence, whichever is longer. It should be noted that the licence in these cases lasts longer than it would in the case of someone over 16: there is no remission for children.

Children not released on licence will be subject to supervision for 12 months, and during that time they may be recalled to detention for up to three months.

The procedures for revocation/recall and re-release are similar to those outlined above.

(b) Children detained after sentence on complaint[1]

Such children are kept at a place determined by the local authority. Their cases must be reviewed every six months in terms of section 20A of the Social Work (Scotland) Act 1968, and may be reviewed at other

1 Criminal Procedure (Scotland) Act 1975, s413, as substituted by the Criminal Justice (Scotland) Act 1987, s59(1).

times. They may be released, either conditionally or unconditionally, at any time provided that a review has been carried out and after having regard to the best interests of the child and the need to protect members of the public. As stressful as the arrangements for release are likely to be for adults and young adults, that pressure is likely to be considerably worse for the child and family going through similar processes. Social workers will already be involved in most of these situations and so can hopefully build upon established relationships to use this period constructively. Here again, the developmental stage and tasks and the particular influence of the child's peer group are liable to be relevant in the social worker's involvement as well as the re-establishment of viable familial relationships.

(4) Law reform

In the Queen's speech in May 1992 the Government announced that they would be bringing forward legislation to give effect to the recommendations of the Kincraig Report[1].

This report suggested that there should be a review of the parole process for lifers and that their licence on release should only last for ten years.

For other prisoners it suggested that parole be abolished for prisoners serving five years or less. Instead these prisoners would automatically be released on completion of half of their sentence, but would be liable to recall for the remainder of the sentence. Recall would be automatic on the commission of an offence which could be tried on indictment and punished by imprisonment. The period of recall would be the unexpired period of sentence at the date of commission of the later offence. There would be no supervision of these prisoners on release; instead the local authority should have a duty to provide advice, guidance and assistance to anyone released from a custodial sentence who asked for it.

Prisoners serving more than five years would be eligible for parole only after serving half of their sentence. The parole board would be obliged to release a prisoner on completion of two-thirds of his/her sentence. Such prisoners would still be subject to social work supervision on release.

In tandem with these reforms of parole the Kincraig Report recommended the abolition of remission. It also suggested that as far as

1 *Parole and Related Issues in Scotland* Cm 598 (1989).

post-release supervision was concerned, young offenders should be in the same position as older prisoners.

9. MENTAL HEALTH AND CRIMINAL LAW

(1) Remand before trial

The High Court and sheriff courts can remand an individual awaiting trial to hospital if they are satisfied, on the basis of evidence from a single doctor, that he/she is suffering from a mental disorder. Before making the order the court must be satisfied that a suitable hospital place is available.

(2) Interim hospital order

After conviction or, in summary cases, where the sheriff is satisfied as to guilt, an interim hospital order can be made. Before making it the court must be satisfied, on the evidence of two doctors, that the offender is suffering from a mental disorder and that it may be appropriate to deal with him/her by way of a hospital order specifying detention in the state hospital. The order lasts for up to 12 weeks, but can be renewed for further 28 day periods up to a maximum of six months. Unless another hospital is specified the offender will go to the state hospital.

(3) Remand for medical examination

Where a court requires further information regarding the physical or mental health of an offender it has the power to order a remand for up to three weeks for medical examination. A condition of the remand will be that the offender must be examined by two doctors. If the remand is not in custody a condition as to residence may be imposed.

(4) Hospital/guardianship orders

These can be made in respect of offenders found guilty of an offence punishable by imprisonment. This qualification, in fact, covers a wide area, as all common law offences, including breach of the peace and other minor offences, are punishable by imprisonment. The orders can only be made by the High Court and the sheriff court. Appropriate cases arising in the district court must be referred to the sheriff court.

Before making a hospital order the court must be satisfied that the grounds for compulsory admission set out in the Mental Health (Scotland) Act 1984 apply to the offender[1]; that a hospital order is the most suitable method of dealing with the case; and that the hospital named in the order will be able to admit the offender within 28 days. If the named hospital is the state hospital the court must be satisfied that the patient cannot be suitably cared for in any other hospital.

Before making a guardianship order the court must be satisfied that the grounds for reception into guardianship specified in the Mental Health (Scotland) Act 1984 apply to the offender[2], and that a guardianship order is the most suitable way of disposing of the case.

The effects of hospital and guardianship orders are, respectively, similar to compulsory detention and guardianship under the Mental Health (Scotland) Act 1984.[3] The main difference is that discharge cannot be ordered by the nearest relative.

(5) Restriction order

The court may attach a restriction order to a hospital order, which may be either unlimited or for a fixed period. A restriction order may be imposed if the court is of the opinion that, having regard to the nature of the offence, the offender's antecedents and the risk of re-offending, it is necessary for the protection of the public from serious harm. As long as the order is in force the offender must be treated as a state patient.

(6) Insanity in bar of trial or as a ground for acquittal

Insanity can operate to prevent an accused going to trial or may be a ground for acquittal. The likely consequence of either occurring in a solemn court is that the accused will be sent to the state hospital and treated as if subject to an unlimited restriction order. Summary courts have more discretion in dealing with such cases.

(7) Transfer of those awaiting trial or sentence

Individuals remanded in custody awaiting trial or sentence may be transferred to hospital. The transfer is made on a transfer order

1 See ch 5, pt 4.
2 See ch 5, pt 5.
3 See ch 5, pts 4 and 5.

granted by a sheriff on the application of the Secretary of State. A transfer order has the effect of a hospital order with an unlimited restriction order.

(8) Transfer of sentenced prisoners

The Secretary of State may make an order transferring prisoners to hospital. Before doing so he/she must be satisfied, on the evidence of two doctors, that the prisoner suffers from a mental disorder. A transfer direction has the same effect as a hospital order and may have added to it a restriction direction having the same effect as a restriction order, though the restriction is limited in time to the unexpired period of sentence.

(9) State patients and the state hospital

A state patient is a patient who cannot be discharged, given leave of absence or transferred without the consent of the Secretary of State, and the authority for whose detention continues indefinitely. There is, however, a right of appeal to the sheriff once every 12 months.

The state hospital is situated at Carstairs and is designed to provide treatment in conditions of special security to patients who have dangerous, violent or criminal propensities.

10. REHABILITATION OF OFFENDERS

All ex-offenders including parolees are subject to the stipulations of the Rehabilitation of Offenders Act 1974 which is a legislative attempt to enable ex-offenders to put their histories behind them. The main exceptions to the law are life imprisonment and sentences of more than 30 months. Once the period of rehabilitation is over, and this involves complex calculations for various sentences but is generally a period of 5, 7 or 10 years which is halved if the offender was under 17 at the time of the offence, then the person is to be treated as if he/she had not committed the offence. He/she need not disclose 'spent' convictions in applying for jobs, making agreements for credit or insurance, or giving evidence in civil proceedings. There are certain exceptions to this which include the disclosure of an offence relating to children or of violence when applying to work for the social work department; when a fine for the conviction is outstanding; when a prohibition or disqualification (as in driving) is in effect for a period longer than the period during which the conviction is spent and in circumstances where there has been royal intervention.

Index